.NET MAUI for C# Developers

Build cross-platform mobile and desktop applications

Jesse Liberty

Rodrigo Juarez

BIRMINGHAM—MUMBAI

.NET MAUI for C# Developers

Group Product Manager: Gebin George

Publishing Product Manager: Kunal Sawant

Senior Editor: Rounak Kulkarni

Technical Editor: Maran Fernandes

Copy Editor: Safis Editing

Project Coordinator: Prajakta Naik

Proofreader: Safis Editing

Indexer: Rekha Nair

Production Designer: Alishon Mendonca

Developer Relations Marketing Executive: Sonia Chauhan and Rayyan Khan

Business Development Executive: Samriddhi Murarka

Production reference: 1170323

Published by Packt Publishing Ltd.

Livery Place

35 Livery Street

Birmingham

B3 2PB, UK.

ISBN 978-1-83763-169-8

www.packtpub.com

To Stacey, Robin, and Rachel. And to Milo, Charlie, Mowgli, Sage, and Simon.

– Jesse Liberty

To all the developers constantly learning and growing; never stop exploring new technologies and expanding your knowledge!

– Rodrigo Juarez

Foreword

I first met Jesse Liberty nearly 5 years ago. I was a PM with a passion for developer tools, new to the .NET world, and jumping right into one of the most ever-changing areas – mobile! At the time, we were still working on .NET MAUI's predecessor, **Xamarin**, and I was shadowing some customer interviews with a colleague to learn the ropes. One of the first interviews we did was with Jesse, for a feature now known and loved as **XAML Hot Reload**. I remember my colleague saying "Oh, this one's with Jesse – he's great. He's been 'around the block' with .NET so he knows what he's talking about, but don't worry. He's really friendly". For me, these "long-time" .NET developers were the most intimidating customers – I would Google their names and see their incredible achievements dating back decades! How was I supposed to ask someone like Jesse meaningful product questions when he's been there for the creation of this whole thing and I *just* started?!

Fortunately, within a few minutes of our call, I could tell how genuinely excited he was to bring someone new into .NET and show them the ropes. He had a passion (and talent!) for teaching, a bunch of different experiences to pull from, and a desire to always keep .NET moving forward so it would continue being the best platform for any developer. Throughout my time in the .NET world, I've met countless amazing community members who have fit this profile (I can happily say I'm *mostly* not intimidated by the long-time .NET folks anymore), but Jesse was one of the first, and that's why, I was so excited when he told me he was writing this book, *.NET MAUI for C# Developers*.

When we decided to build .NET MAUI, we wanted to accomplish 2 things: bring mobile into the first-party, full .NET ecosystem (no more separate runtimes or tools or confusing slides!) and fix a bunch of the stuff Xamarin developers complained about but couldn't be addressed with the existing platform. Jesse was one of those Xamarin developers, and when we shared the idea with him and other Microsoft MVPs, he was one of the first to share his excitement. When we shipped GA, Jesse started a blog series *Learning .NET MAUI*, where he took his readers along with him as he became familiar with the platform for the first time. Jesse has also regularly discussed .NET MAUI on his podcast, *Yet Another Podcast*, from our earliest days to the latest and greatest releases.

Jesse has been an author in .NET and adjacent communities for nearly 2 decades, and there is no one better suited to get C# developers to build native mobile and desktop apps with .NET MAUI. Even if you're new to C#, you will learn a *LOT* from this book and will enjoy Jesse's approachable and honest writing. He takes you through the basics, from getting set up with Visual Studio to building your UI and navigation, and even consuming RESTful APIs. With one codebase, a computer, and this book in hand, you're well on your way to becoming a cross-platform developer with .NET MAUI. I can't wait to see what you build!

Maddy Montaquila (Leger)

Senior Product Manager, .NET MAUI, Microsoft

Contributors

About the authors

Jesse Liberty specializes in C#, .NET MAUI, and Git. He is a certified Xamarin developer, a Xamarin MVP, and a Microsoft MVP.

Liberty hosts the popular *Yet Another Podcast* (jesseliberty.com) and he is the author of more than a dozen best-selling programming books (http://surl.li/fljbq).

Jesse was a technical evangelist for Microsoft, a distinguished software engineer at AT&T, a software architect for PBS, and vice president of information technology at Citibank, and he was on the teaching staff at Brandeis University.

He is a recognized expert and has spoken at conferences worldwide.

To contact Jesse, see his **Find Me** page at https://jesseliberty.com/find-me.

Rodrigo Juarez is a full stack and Xamarin/MAUI developer. He has over 25 years of experience in a wide variety of projects in the development of applications for web, desktop, and mobile using Microsoft technologies in areas such as management, services, insurance, pharmacy, health, and banking.

About the reviewers

Daniel Brevitt is a seasoned software developer with over 15 years of experience in .NET development. With a focus on mobile app development, Daniel has worked extensively with Xamarin and is passionate about creating high-quality cross-platform mobile solutions and helping others learn to do the same.

Tidjani Belmansour is a cloud solutions architect and the director of the Azure Center of Excellence for Cofomo, a leader in IT consulting services in Canada. Tidjani is also a Microsoft Azure MVP since 2019 and the co-organizer of the Azure Quebec Community.

He holds a bachelor's degree in computer science and a Ph.D. in industrial engineering. He started his computer journey in 1988 and has held various positions including that of a developer, software architect, and cloud architect.

Tidjani is also an international speaker and a book reviewer and has authored two of the articles in *"97 Things Every Cloud Engineer Should Know"* (O'Reilly editions).

You can find Tidjani on Twitter (@tidjani_b) and LinkedIn (https://www.linkedin.com/in/tidjani-belmansour).

Table of Contents

6

Layout   127

Part 2 – Intermediate Topics

7

Understanding Navigation   149

8

Storing and Retrieving Data   171

9

Unit Testing   185

Part 3 – Advanced Topics

10

Consuming REST Services 209

11

Exploring Advanced Topics 245

Assessments   263

Index   267

Other Books You May Enjoy   274

Preface

.NET MAUI is Microsoft's cross-platform development framework for building iOS, Android, Windows, Mac, and Tizen apps. With .NET MAUI, you build the UI and the logic once and emit native code for each platform. It is the successor technology to **Xamarin.Forms** and adds powerful new features and capabilities.

The .NET MAUI Community Toolkit supplements .NET MAUI to provide source code generators, behaviors, and much more, greatly enhancing and extending .NET MAUI as the premier development framework for building applications.

Who this book is for

This book is targeted at anyone who has a fundamental understanding of C# and wishes to write cross-platform applications. If you are not a C# programmer but have experience with another object-oriented program, you should have no trouble following the examples.

What this book covers

Chapter 1, Assembling Your Tools and Creating Your First App, shows you how to download the (free) software you need and will teach you how to create an "out-of-the-box" app to see what is provided to get you started.

Chapter 2, What We Will Build – Forget Me Not, introduces our non-trivial, real-world app – "Forget Me Not." We'll go over what it does and then we'll walk through the various pages to see the entire completed project that we'll be working on for the rest of the book.

Chapter 3, XAML and Fluent C#, explores the markup language used to create the UI of a .NET MAUI app. We'll also examine how you can write the UI in C# if you prefer.

Chapter 4, MVVM and Controls, examines the most popular and powerful architecture for building .NET MAUI apps – **Model-View-ViewModel** (**MVVM**). We'll also take a look at many of the core controls used to create the UI.

Chapter 5, Advanced Controls, builds on the previous chapter, adding more advanced controls to create a more powerful and robust UI.

Chapter 6, Layout, focuses on the techniques to arrange the controls on your view and create a professional appearance.

Chapter 7, Understanding Navigation, shows how you move from one page to another and how you can pass along data as you navigate. No serious .NET MAUI app has only one page.

Chapter 8, Storing and Retrieving Data, explores the two ways to persist data. The first is useful for storing a user's preferences for the program. The second involves building a relational database using SQLite.

Chapter 9, Unit Testing, shows how to use xUnit and the mocking tool **nSubstitute** to create powerful unit tests. No .NET MAUI program is complete without an extensive suite of unit tests to ensure a program is working correctly.

Chapter 10, Consuming REST Services, explores how to validate a user's login and obtain their data from Azure. Many modern apps get their data from the cloud, and the most popular way to do so is by using REST services.

Chapter 11, Exploring Advanced Topics, moves into expert techniques, such as managing visual states, using behaviors and triggers, and selecting data templates at run time.

To get the most out of this book

You will want to have at least fundamental experience with an object-oriented language, especially C#. You do not need to know the latest advances in C#, and the example code is explained in depth. You will want the latest version of Visual Studio; the Community Edition is free and will work fine. If you are on a Mac (or Linux), the examples should work fine with Visual Studio for Mac, although they were not developed on a Mac.

Software/hardware covered in the book	Operating system requirements
.NET MAUI	Windows, macOS, or Linux
.NET MAUI Community Toolkit	Windows, macOS, or Linux

Install Visual Studio (or Visual Studio for Mac) from `https://visualstudio.com`. Do not mistake it for Visual Studio Code, which is a different editor.

If you are using the digital version of this book, we advise you to type the code yourself or access it from the book's GitHub repository (a link is available in the next section). Doing so will help you avoid any potential errors related to the copying and pasting of code.

Please note that there is only one repository, with branches for each chapter. The branch represents the code for the completed chapter. If you wish to follow along, start with the branch from the previous chapter.

Download the example code files

You can download the example code files for this book from GitHub at `https://github.com/PacktPublishing/.NET-MAUI-for-C-Sharp-Developers`. If there's an update to the code, it will be updated in the GitHub repository.

We also have other code bundles from our rich catalog of books and videos available at `https://github.com/PacktPublishing/`. Check them out!

Download the color images

We also provide a PDF file that has color images of the screenshots and diagrams used in this book. You can download it here: `https://packt.link/z75ye`.

Conventions used

There are a number of text conventions used throughout this book.

`Code in text`: Indicates code words in text, database table names, folder names, filenames, file extensions, pathnames, dummy URLs, user input, and Twitter handles. Here is an example: "Mount the downloaded `WebStorm-10*.dmg` disk image file as another disk in your system."

A block of code is set as follows:

```
<VerticalStackLayout x:Name="LoginStackLayout">
    <HorizontalStackLayout WidthRequest="300">
        <Label
            Style="{StaticResource LargeLabel}"
            Text="User Name" />
```

When we wish to draw your attention to a particular part of a code block, the relevant lines or items are set in bold:

```
<Entry
            HorizontalOptions="End"
            Placeholder="User Name"
            Text="{Binding Name}"
            WidthRequest="150" />
```

Bold: Indicates a new term, an important word, or words that you see on screen. For instance, words in menus or dialog boxes appear in **bold**. Here is an example: "To get started, install the latest version of the **sqlite-net-pcl** NuGet package, as shown in *Figure 8.2*."

> **Tips or important notes**
> Appear like this.

Get in touch

Feedback from our readers is always welcome.

General feedback: If you have questions about any aspect of this book, email us at customercare@ packtpub.com and mention the book title in the subject of your message.

Errata: Although we have taken every care to ensure the accuracy of our content, mistakes do happen. If you have found a mistake in this book, we would be grateful if you would report this to us. Please visit www.packtpub.com/support/errata and fill in the form.

Piracy: If you come across any illegal copies of our works in any form on the internet, we would be grateful if you would provide us with the location address or website name. Please contact us at copyright@packt.com with a link to the material.

If you are interested in becoming an author: If there is a topic that you have expertise in and you are interested in either writing or contributing to a book, please visit authors.packtpub.com.

Share Your Thoughts

Once you've read *.Net MAUI for C# Developers*, we'd love to hear your thoughts! Scan the QR code below to go straight to the Amazon review page for this book and share your feedback.

https://packt.link/r/1837631697

Your review is important to us and the tech community and will help us make sure we're delivering excellent quality content.

Download a free PDF copy of this book

Thanks for purchasing this book!

Do you like to read on the go but are unable to carry your print books everywhere?

Is your eBook purchase not compatible with the device of your choice?

Don't worry, now with every Packt book you get a DRM-free PDF version of that book at no cost.

Read anywhere, any place, on any device. Search, copy, and paste code from your favorite technical books directly into your application.

The perks don't stop there, you can get exclusive access to discounts, newsletters, and great free content in your inbox daily

Follow these simple steps to get the benefits:

1. Scan the QR code or visit the link below

https://packt.link/free-ebook/9781837631698

2. Submit your proof of purchase

3. That's it! We'll send your free PDF and other benefits to your email directly

Part 1 – Getting Started

In this part, we will get you set up with the required software and examine the project we're going to build. We'll then go on to examine XAML – the markup language for .NET MAUI. Next, we'll take a deep look at MVVM, the architecture for it and most .NET MAUI apps, and we'll undertake an extensive review of the controls and structures used to build the user interface.

This part has the following chapters:

- *Chapter 1, Assembling Your Tools and Creating Your First App*
- *Chapter 2, What We Will Build – Forget Me Not*
- *Chapter 3, XAML and Fluent C#*
- *Chapter 4, MVVM and Controls*
- *Chapter 5, Advanced Controls*
- *Chapter 6, Layout*

1
Assembling Your Tools and Creating Your First App

In this book, we'll be building iOS, Android, Windows, and Mac applications using one common code base. Everything you need is free unless you want to build for iOS and Mac, in which case you need a Mac computer. I'm going to assume you have a Mac, but if you don't, very little will change; you'll just be more limited in the platforms you can deploy to.

> **An alternative if you don't have a Mac**
>
> James Montemagno of Microsoft has a workaround video if you don't have a Mac. There are severe limitations, but needs must. My personal recommendation is that if you don't have a Mac, do your development with Android. Here's the video: https://www.youtube.com/watch?v=snQ1C6Cppr8.

In the coming chapters, you will see a non-trivial .NET MAUI project that we will build incrementally. Along the way, we will examine how to create the **User Interface** (**UI**) with **XAML** (a markup language) and **C#**.

> **MAUI Blazor**
>
> An alternative, not covered in this book, is to use MAUI Blazor, which allows you to create a cross-platform application using your Blazor skills. You can learn more about MAUI Blazor at https://bit.ly/MauiBlazor.

In the first part of the book, we will discuss the principal architecture for .NET MAUI: **Model-View-ViewModel** (**MVVM**). We will then dive into the diverse controls available for creating powerful UIs followed by a chapter dedicated to techniques for laying out these controls on the page.

We will move on to discussing the Shell navigation architecture and how you move from page to page, passing along data as needed. We'll look at persisting data and then stop to discuss the all-important topic of testing your code.

While .NET MAUI provides a cornucopia of controls, there are times when you need something that Microsoft did not anticipate, so we'll dedicate a chapter to creating custom controls. (Once you have a custom control, you can use it in any subsequent .NET MAUI projects you work on.)

In the final section of the book, we'll look at consuming a REST API and creating a web frontend to the same REST API we used for the mobile and desktop applications, this time using **Blazor**.

In this chapter, you will learn how to get and install Visual Studio for writing the program and Git for managing and safeguarding your code. Each chapter's final code will be in a dedicated branch, with the final product in the main branch.

In this chapter, you will find the following:

- A description of Visual Studio, along with installation instructions
- A description of Git, along with installation instructions
- A description of how to create your first, out-of-the-box program, and a tour of the files in that project

> **App versus application**
> Since we will be building for iOS and Android (which refer to apps) and also Windows and Mac (which refer to applications), I'll be using the two terms interchangeably.

Let's get the software you need, and then set up Visual Studio.

Technical requirements

To follow along with this chapter and book, you will need to obtain and install Visual Studio and Git. To do this, you will need a Windows machine (Windows 10 or later). In addition, if you want to write for iOS and/or the Mac, you will need an Apple computer on the same network as your Windows computer.

All of the code in this book is available at https://github.com/PacktPublishing/.NET-MAUI-for-C-Sharp-Developers. The code for each chapter will have its own branch and that will be noted in the *Technical requirements* section of the given chapter. Note that there is no code for *Chapters 1* and *2*.

> **A word on Visual Studio Mac**
>
> It should be possible to follow along with this book using Visual Studio Mac, but some of the menus and certainly many of the keystrokes will be different. In my experience, Visual Studio Mac follows Visual Studio with a short delay in the implementation of new features. If all you have is a Mac, by all means do your development there. If you have both, or just a Windows machine, you'll find it a bit easier to follow along with Visual Studio (for Windows).
>
> While I'm at it, I'll mention that I'm using Windows 11 on a desktop computer with 64 GB of memory and a 1 TB disk. None of that is required for this book. You will want at least 16 GB of memory for .NET MAUI programming.

Getting and installing Visual Studio

The first and foremost software you'll need for this book is the latest version of Visual Studio from Microsoft. You can, of course, write .NET and .NET MAUI apps with any number of editors and/or **Integrated Development Environments (IDEs)**, but Visual Studio is what I'll be using in this book because it is, I believe, the most powerful IDE for the job. All the examples will use Visual Studio and your job will be much easier if you do so as well, at least while working your way through this book.

To get Visual Studio, open a browser and navigate to `https://visualstudio.microsoft.com/`. Microsoft changes the appearance of this page pretty frequently, but you should see the opportunity to download **Visual Studio**, **Visual Studio for Mac**, and **Visual Studio Code**.

Installing Visual Studio

On the website, click on **Download Visual Studio**. You can download whichever version you prefer. Note that the Community Version is free. If you already have Visual Studio 2022 or later installed, you need not add another copy, though they will run side by side assuming you have enough disk space. For installation, follow these steps:

1. Once Visual Studio has been downloaded, click on the executable to begin the installation process. The installer will update and you will be presented with the **Workloads** dialog box as shown in *Figure 1.1*.

Figure 1.1 – Visual Studio Workloads

2. Visual Studio lets you pick and choose what workloads you'll need so that it is no bigger than necessary. Be sure to check **Azure development**, **.NET Multi-platform App UI development**, and **.NET desktop development** as shown in *Figure 1.2.*

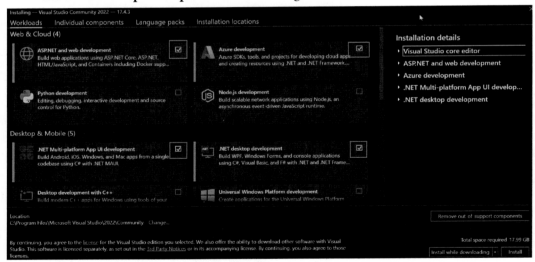

Figure 1.2 – Selecting workloads

3. Next, click **Install** and get yourself a cup of coffee; this may take a few minutes. You should see progress in the Visual Studio installer, as in *Figure 1.3.*

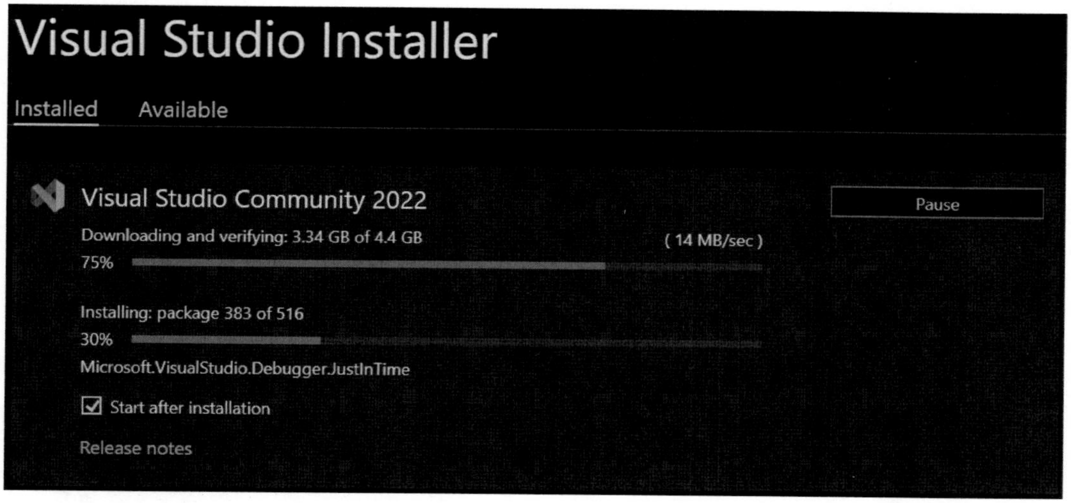

Figure 1.3 – Visual Studio Installer

When the installation is complete, Visual Studio will open.

> **A word on ReSharper**
>
> **ReSharper** is a very powerful tool that greatly enhances productivity for .NET developers. It is not free, however, and while I use it every day in my own work, we'll not be using it in this book. Since we can do everything in Visual Studio without ReSharper (though it may take a few more keystrokes), no harm done.

With Visual Studio installed, the only remaining issue is storing, safeguarding, and retrieving the source code. For that, we'll use **Git** – the industry standard. The final application will be in the main branch, with each chapter's code being in a dedicated branch.

Git

The next software you need is Git. To download Git, navigate to `git-scm.com/download` and choose your operating system. I'll choose Windows. Next, I'll choose **64-bit Git for Windows Setup** under **Standalone Installer**. This will cause an immediate download. Double-click on the downloaded file to install it. If you already have Git installed, this will update it.

You do not need any of the Git GUIs, as we'll be interacting with Git through Visual Studio.

When the installation is complete, you'll see the following options: **Launch Git Bash** and **View the release notes**. Uncheck both and click on **Finish**.

Let's continue with our exploration of Visual Studio.

Opening Visual Studio

You'll need to obtain the rest of the software from within Visual Studio, so let's open that next. If the installation went as expected, the launch dialog will be on the screen:

1. Click on **Create a new project**. (If you've been brought directly into Visual Studio, bypassing the launch dialog, just click **File | New Project**.)

2. It is now time to pick the template we want. Templates make getting started easier. In the **Search for Templates** box, enter MAUI. A few choices will be presented; you want **.NET MAUI App**, as shown in the following figure:

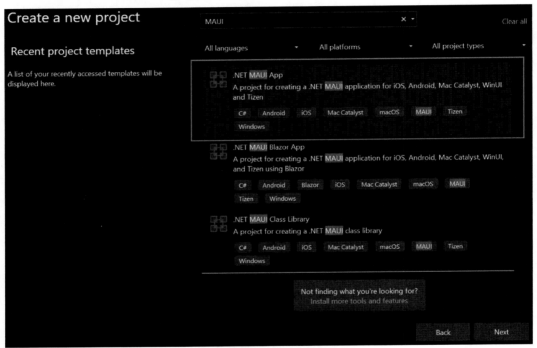

Figure 1.4 – Creating a new project

3.   Click **Next**. Here we give our project a name. The first project we're going to create is not
     ForgetMeNotDemo (the project that you will be building as part of this book), but rather a
     sample project just to take a quick look around. Name it something creative such as SampleApp
     and place it in a location on your disk where you will be able to easily find it later. Before clicking
     Next, make sure your dialog looks similar to *Figure 1.5*.

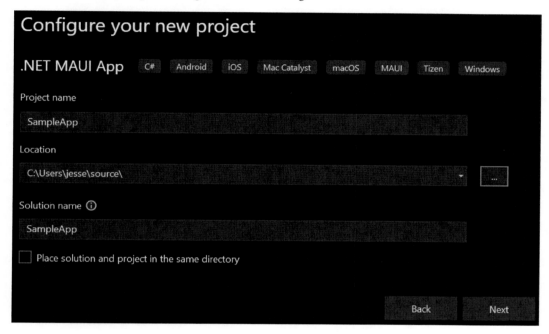

Figure 1.5 – Naming your project

4.   Click **Next** and use the dropdown to choose the latest version of .NET. At the time of writing,
     that is .NET 7. Finally, click on **Create**.

> **Note**
>
> Because Microsoft is always updating Visual Studio, your screens or steps may vary slightly.
> Don't let that worry you. The version I am using is Visual Studio 2022, version 17.4.3. As long
> as yours is the same or later, you're all set. But just to be sure, let's launch the sample app (*F5*).
> You should see something that looks like *Figure 1.6*.

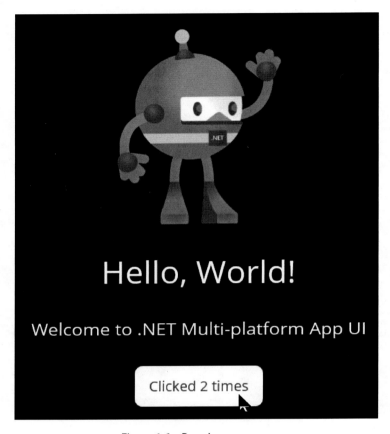

Figure 1.6 – Running your app

5.   On the screen that you see in the preceding figure, click the button a couple times to make sure it is working.

Generally speaking, I will not be walking through how to do simple things on Visual Studio. The assumption is that you are a C# programmer and so you are probably familiar with Visual Studio. On the other hand, on the off chance that you are not, I'll describe how to do anything that is not immediately intuitive. Next, let's explore the out-of-the-box app in a bit more detail.

Quick tour of the app

Let's take a quick tour to see what comes with an out-of-the-box app. First, stop the app by pressing the red square button in the menu bar. Make sure **Solution Explorer** is open (if not, go to **View | Solution Explorer**). Notice that there are three folders and four files, as shown in *Figure 1.7*:

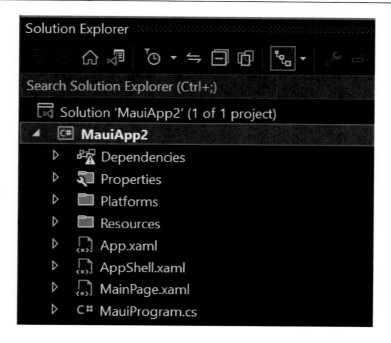

Figure 1.7 – Three folders and four files

The files with the .xaml extension are XAML files – that is, they use the XAML markup language. I will not assume you know XAML, and in fact, throughout this book, I will provide layout and other code in both XAML and fluent C#, but that is for the next chapter.

Right now, let's open this out of the box project.

This is the entry point for the program. As you can see, it is a static class with a static method that is responsible for creating the app itself. We'll come back to this file in subsequent chapters.

When you open MainPage.xaml, you will see a layout with controls for the page we just looked at (with the goofy MAUI guy waving and counting our button clicks). Again, we're going to come back to layout and controls, but scan this page and see whether you can guess what is going on. You may find that it isn't as alien as it seemed at first glance. You can, if you are so motivated, learn quite a bit about XAML just by reading this page carefully.

Click on the triangle next to MainPage.xaml to reveal the code-behind file. Code-behind files are always named <PageName>.xaml.cs – in this case, MainPage.xaml.cs. These files are always in C#. Here, we see the constructor and then an event handler. When the user clicks on the button, this event handler (OnCounterClicked) is called.

By flipping back and forth between the XAML and the code-behind file, you may be able to figure out how the button works and how the count of clicks is displayed. No need to do this, however, as we'll be covering all these details in upcoming chapters.

At the moment, most of the other files are nearly empty and not worth the time to examine.

Just for fun, expand the `Resources` folder. You'll see that there are folders for the application icon, fonts, images, and so forth. All the resources for all of the platforms are kept here.

Then there is a `Platforms` folder, which contains whatever is needed on a per-platform basis. For example, iOS applications require an `info.plist` file, which you'll find in **Platforms | iOS**.

There is much more to see in a .NET MAUI application, but we will tackle each part as we build Forget Me Not™.

Summary

In this chapter, you saw how to find, download, and install Visual Studio and Git, the two tools you'll need throughout the book. You also created your first .NET MAUI app, and we walked through some of its files, albeit quickly.

In the next chapter, we'll take an extended look at XAML: the markup language for page layout and the creation of controls. We'll then look at creating layouts and controls in C# and a new library that allows us to use Fluent C# to create layouts and controls.

Quiz

Test your understanding of this chapter by answering the following questions:

1. How do you create a new project?
2. How do you find **Solution Explorer** if it is not visible?
3. What does the `.xaml` extension indicate?
4. What do we call the `.cs` file associated with an `.xaml` file?
5. Where is the entry point for a .NET MAUI app?

You try it

Most chapters will have a *You try it* section, in which you will be encouraged to take on a task related to what was covered in the chapter. Alas, this chapter does not have a task for you.

2

What We Will Build: Forget Me Not

During the course of this book, we will build the core of a complete non-trivial application called *Forget Me Not*. It is easiest to get somewhere when you know where you are going, so this chapter will review the finished product from a user's point of view. That is, in this chapter, we'll review the functionality, and in subsequent chapters, we'll dive into the implementation.

Technical requirements

This chapter does not review code (although all the subsequent ones will) and so there are no particular technical requirements for this chapter.

What is Forget Me Not?

Forget Me Not™ is an application designed to help you buy presents for your buddies and to allow them to easily buy presents for you.

The core of Forget Me Not is your list of preferences, as shown in *Figure 2.1*:

Figure 2.1 – Preferences

You fill in each field with whatever and however much information you like. What's more, you can change the prompt on the left and then fill in your new preference on the right! This gives you the maximum flexibility in specifying your preferences and your taste in various potential present categories.

The power of this is seen once you have Buddies.

Buddies

If a friend or relative has the app, you can invite them to be your Buddy. Once your relationship is established in the cloud-based database, you can see your Buddy's preferences, and they can see yours (though you cannot edit each other's preferences).

Inviting Buddies

To invite a Buddy, you navigate, using the tabs, to the Buddy list and tap on **Add Buddy**, which will bring up the **Share** page, as shown in *Figure 2.2*.

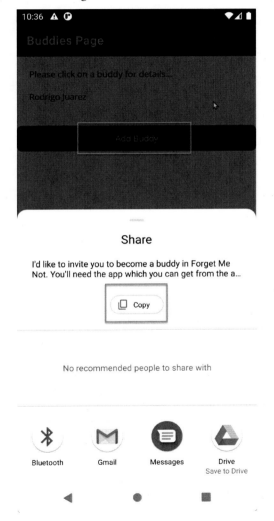

Figure 2.2 – The Share page

You can now use any of the platform-specific share options, including copying the invitation. Let's send it as an email message, as shown in *Figure 2.3*.

Invitation   _ ⤢ ✕

Rodrigo Juarez (rodrigomjuarez@gmail.com)

Invitation

I'd like to invite you to become a buddy in Forget Me Not. You'll need the app which you can get from the app store. Once you have it set up, click on this link:

https://magic link goes here

That will establish us as buddies, and you can see my preferences. Don't forget to set up your preferences so that I can see them when I want to get you a present.

Hope you will join me.

Figure 2.3 – Email invitation

The text of the invitation is canned and automatically provided, but the user can edit it at will. The *magic link* will be provided by the server for one-time access to the login page, to reciprocate the connection to the inviting Buddy. Note that this will not be covered in this book as this work is done by the API.

Those are the key pages, but there are a couple of others.

Other pages

In addition to these primary pages, there is an **About** page, as shown in the following figure:

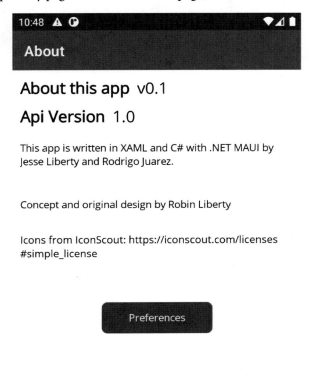

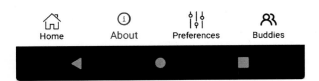

Figure 2.4 – About page

Clicking on **Preferences** here brings up the **User Preferences** page, as shown in *Figure 2.5*.

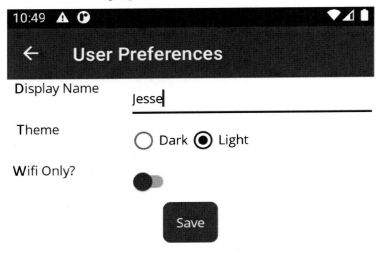

Figure 2.5 – User Preferences

There isn't that much more to the app. While there are only half a dozen pages, those pages do a lot and will provide fertile ground for learning the basics and then going way beyond the essentials to cover intermediate and then advanced topics.

What you'll learn

Even just these few pages will give us an opportunity to discuss virtually every aspect of .NET MAUI, including the following:

- Shell navigation
- Layout
- XAML
- Controls
- Displaying collections
- The MVVM pattern
- Data binding
- Persisting data
- Consuming REST services
- Advanced topics in managing the UI

- Use of the Community Toolkit

- Behaviors

- Triggers

By the time you're finished reading this book, you will have two things: a working application and expertise in building .NET MAUI apps!

Summary

In the coming chapters, we'll be building the Forget Me Not app as described in this chapter. The implementation of this seemingly simple app will allow us to explore core aspects of .NET MAUI and then move on to intermediate and ultimately advanced topics.

As mentioned in *Chapter 1*, each chapter (except this one) will end with a quiz to ensure that you are comfortable with what was covered and a *You try it* section where you will be encouraged to put your new skills to the test.

I can't wait to get started. Let's begin with examining the markup language (XAML) and using C# for the logic of our program.

3
XAML and Fluent C#

In this chapter, we will look at how .NET MAUI applications are created using a markup language for the user interface and C# for all the logic.

.NET MAUI programs are (typically) written in two languages. One is C#, which is used for all the logic, and the other is **XAML** (pronounced *zamel*, to rhyme with camel), which is used for the layout and creation of controls. As you'll see, the use of XAML is optional. You can create your layout and controls all in C#, but most people don't. However, that may be changing (more and more of the Microsoft Learn documentation shows both ways).

When might you choose to use C#?

There are a few reasons to use C# instead of XAML, not least that you know C# and don't want to bother learning XAML. If you do this, however, you'll find it difficult to read other people's code, as most existing Xamarin.Forms (the precursor to .NET MAUI) apps are written with XAML.

Using C# can assist in those situations where the design should change based on some condition (such as the type of data you get at runtime). But there are other ways to handle that with XAML as explained in *Chapter 11, Advanced Topics.*

This book will show C# for some pages, but the focus will be on XAML.

All of the Microsoft documentation is at least in XAML; only some is in C# and some is in Fluent C# (a topic we'll take up later in this chapter). Nearly all **Xamarin.Forms** applications and samples use XAML and, for that reason alone, it is worth learning. More important, XAML is a highly expressive declarative markup language that makes creating layouts and controls if not easy, then at least manageable.

This chapter will cover the following topics:

- Understanding the structure of XAML
- Code-behind and event handlers
- Exploring the layout options
- Creating the UI in C#

Technical requirements

To follow along with this chapter, you will need the following:

- Visual Studio version 17.5 or later (it's best to update to the latest version)
- The source code covered in this chapter can be found in the GitHub repository: `https://github.com/PacktPublishing/.NET-MAUI-for-C-Sharp-Developers/tree/XAMLAndCSharp`

Understanding the structure of XAML

XAML files have the `.xaml` extension, for example, `MainPage.xaml`, in the out-of-the-box program as shown in *Chapter 1*. Let's examine this file to explore XAML for its layout and declaration of controls.

> **Just an overview**
>
> This chapter will only scratch the surface of creating XAML layout and controls. *Chapter 4* and *Chapter 5* will cover the details on controls and layouts, respectively.

A .NET MAUI page that is written in XAML will have a name in the format `MyName.xaml`, and associated with that page will be a code-behind page (explained shortly) in the format `MyName.xaml.cs`.

At the top of the XAML page is a declaration that this file is, in reality, an XML-type file. That declaration must be at the very top of every `.xaml` file.

There are different types of pages (also called views). The most common is `ContentPage`, and here `MainPage` is created as `ContentPage` using this code:

```
<?xml version="1.0" encoding="utf-8" ?>
<ContentPage xmlns="http://schemas.microsoft.com/
  dotnet/2021/maui"
    xmlns:x="http://schemas.microsoft.com/winfx/2009/xaml"
      x:Class="ForgetMeNotDemo.View.MainPage">
```

As part of the declaration of ContentPage, we identify two namespaces (xmlns). The first namespace is unnamed and is for .NET MAUI itself. The second namespace, named x, is for XAML.

Finally, the class that this XAML file is part of is ForgetMeNotDemo.View.MainPage.

The first part (ForgetMeNotDemo.View) is the namespace, and MainPage is the name of the class. The View part is added to indicate the folder under the project.

Associated with every .xaml page is a code-behind page, as mentioned earlier. It is possible to put the logic of your program in the code-behind, which is what we will do for this chapter (in the next chapter, we'll look at an alternative that is better for testing). In any case, there are a few things that must go in the code-behind, as you'll see in the next section.

The code-behind file

Every XAML file has an associated code-behind page whose name is in the format <pagename>.xaml.cs. Thus, the code-behind for this page is MainPage.xaml.cs.

The code-behind file is typically (and correctly) named after the class (that is, the MainPage class will be in MainPage.xaml and MainPage.xaml.cs). The namespace is explicitly declared in the file and should follow the folder structure. Thus, if the namespace is ForgetMeNotDemo/MainPage, then we'd expect MainPage.cs to have the ForGetMeNotDemo namespace:

```
namespace ForgetMeNotDemo.View;
public partial class MainPage : ContentPage
```

Notice that this is a partial class. In .NET MAUI, all UI classes are marked partial. Notice also that the class indicates that it is ContentPage, which is consistent with what we saw in the XAML.

In addition to defining classes, you can use XAML to create the layout of the page, that is, where things go in relation to one another. XAML provides a number of layout options as described next.

Exploring the layout options

Returning to MainPage.xaml, the first thing we see below ContentPage is a ScrollView layout element. This is a layout that essentially says that anything contained in ScrollView can (surprise!) scroll.

A layout contains other layouts and controls. It does this just as it's done in XML, which is with opening and closing tags. Here is the syntax:

```
<ScrollView>
    // … layouts and controls
</ScrollView>
```

A page can have only one element. Typically, that element is a layout, and since layouts can contain other layouts and controls, an entire hierarchy can be created.

The top four elements in `MainPage.xaml` (out of the box) are as follows:

```
<ScrollView>   [1]
    <VerticalStackLayout    [2]
        Spacing="25"
        Padding="30,0"
        VerticalOptions="Center">

        <Image [3]
            Source="dotnet_bot.png"
            SemanticProperties.Description="Cute dot net
                bot waving hi to you!"
            HeightRequest="200"
            HorizontalOptions="Center" />

        <Label [4]
            Text="Hello, World!"
            SemanticProperties.HeadingLevel="Level1"
            FontSize="32"
            HorizontalOptions="Center" />
</ScrollView>
```

> **Why is this code different from what is in the repo?**
> The preceding code is what you get out of the box. In this chapter, we will enhance this code, and the repo reflects the finished version as of the end of the chapter.

Let's take this one element at a time. We've already discussed the first element, ScrollView, so let's start with the next, that is, VerticalStackLayout.

VerticalStackLayout

Inside ScrollView is VerticalStackLayout. As the name implies, this layout holds things stacked one on top of another. Here, we have defined three properties for VerticalStackLayout: Spacing, Padding, and VerticalOptions. Now, VerticalStackLayout has dozens of properties and methods. We will learn more about this in *Chapter 5, Layouts*.

`Spacing` determines the amount of vertical space there is between each of the contained elements. Here, `Spacing` is set to 25 **device-independent units (DIPs)**. Using DIPs means that you can define the size for one device (phone, Windows, and so on) and have it look as you intend on all other devices. At least that's the theory. As a good friend once said, "In theory, theory and practice are the same. But in practice, they never are."

The second property is `Padding`. This is one of the ways you can control the position and alignment of your controls. The second principal way is with `Margins`. This tells you the distance from the nearest other element (or from the edge of the page), whereas `Padding` tells you the size of the buffer around the current element, as shown in *Figure 3.1*:

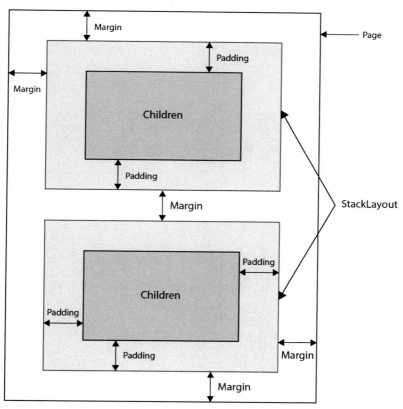

Figure 3.1 – Padding and Margin

`Padding` is written in the format *left, top, right, bottom*. A `Padding` value of (20,10,5,0) would have a padding on the left of 20 DIPs, 10 on the top, 5 on the right, and no DIPs on the bottom. If the top and bottom are the same, they can be combined. The same is true for the right and left. Thus, as we have here, `Padding = "30,0"`, which means that the left and right will have a padding of 30 but there will be no padding on the top and bottom.

The final property in `VerticalStackLayout` is `VerticalOptions`, which indicates where to place `VerticalStackLayout` with respect to its container (in this case, `ScrollView`). The options for this are based on an enumeration:

- *Center*
- *End*
- *Fill*
- *Start*

This enumeration is used with a number of different layouts and controls. For now, it is enough to know that *Start* means *top* for vertical layouts and *far left* for horizontal. Similarly, *End* means *far right* for horizontal and *bottom* for vertical. We'll return to these values later in the book.

Image

The third element of the page is an `Image` element, which in this case has four properties. The first is the source (where to find the image). The second is called `SemanticProperties.Description`. **Semantic properties** are added to assist those who use screen readers.

You cannot set the height directly (it is read only), but you can set `HeightRequest`, which we have done here to `200` DIPs. .NET MAUI will try to provide that height depending on your other settings on the page and the available space. Finally, we set `HorizontalOptions` to `Center` so that we center the image on the horizontal axis.

Label

Next, we see `Label`. In this case, it too has four properties. The first is the text to display on the label. The second is, again, for screen readers, indicating the organizational structure (here the label is at the top level). The third property is `FontSize`. There are a couple of ways to set `FontSize`, as we'll see in *Chapter 4*, but here we are using DIPs. Finally, once again, we set `HorizontalOptions` to `Center`.

If you scroll down the page, you'll see there is another `Label` and a `Button` control (which does pretty much what you'd guess).

At the bottom, you will see the close for `VerticalStackLayout`, then the close for `ScrollView`, and finally the close for `ContentPage` itself.

The XAML thus provides a highly structured approach to describing the layout. Here is the complete XAML page:

```
<?xml version="1.0" encoding="utf-8" ?>
<ContentPage
    x:Class="ForgetMeNotDemo.MainPage"
    xmlns="http://schemas.microsoft.com/dotnet/2021/maui"
    xmlns:x="http://schemas.microsoft.com/winfx/2009/xaml">

    <ScrollView>
        <VerticalStackLayout
            Padding="30,0"
            Spacing="25"
            VerticalOptions="Center">

            <Image
                HeightRequest="200"
                HorizontalOptions="Center"
                SemanticProperties.Description="Cute dot
                    net bot waving hi to you!"
                Source="dotnet_bot.png" />

            <Label
                FontSize="32"
                HorizontalOptions="Center"
                SemanticProperties.HeadingLevel="Level1"
                Text="Hello, World!" />

            <Label
                FontSize="18"
                HorizontalOptions="Center"
                SemanticProperties.Description="
                    Welcome to dot net Multi platform
                        App U I"
                SemanticProperties.HeadingLevel="Level2"
                Text="Welcome to .NET Multi-platform
                    App UI" />
```

```
            <Button
                x:Name="CounterBtn"
                Clicked="OnCounterClicked"
                HorizontalOptions="Center"
                SemanticProperties.Hint="Counts the number
                    of times you click"
                Text="Click me" />

        </VerticalStackLayout>
    </ScrollView>
</ContentPage>
```

This page opens by declaring `ContentPage` (the most common type of page) and defines the namespace and name of the page (which will be reflected in the code-behind as well). It then declares two standard namespaces (using `xmlns`), the first for .NET MAUI and the second for the XAML markup.

We see `ScrollView`, and inside of that, we see `VerticalStackLayout`, which is set to use padding and spacing and to be centered vertically. We'll review these properties as we go along.

`VerticalStackout` contains four controls: an image, two labels, and a button. Each of these controls has its own properties. You do not have to be concerned about these properties now; they are explained later. The takeaway here is that layouts can contain layouts and controls. They stack like Ukrainian dolls, one within the other (though controls do not contain controls).

Notes

Each `ContentPage` can have only one layout, but that layout can contain other layouts (as we see here), and so that is not a troublesome problem.

Also, note that due to the size restriction of the printed page, some text will wrap to the next line.

You can even do this in Visual Studio by going to **Tools | Options | C# | General** and checking the box for **Word wrap**. If you do this, I recommend also checking **Show visual glyphs for word wrap**, which makes reading the code easier. While you are there, you may want to check **Line numbers**, which can come in very handy, especially when tracking down compile errors. These options are shown in *Figure 3.2*.

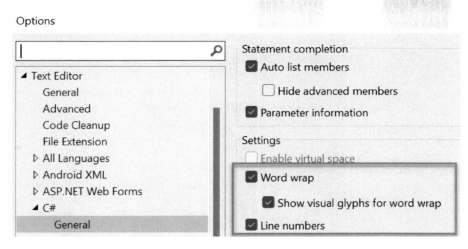

Figure 3.2 – Setting Word wrap and Line numbers

Now, when your line of code is too wide to display, it will wrap and you'll see a small arrow on the right side indicating that the line has continued, as shown in *Figure 3.3*.

Figure 3.3 – Visual Studio word wrap

When something happens such as the user clicking a button, an event is raised. The event is handled in the code-behind, which we'll review next.

> **Events versus commands**
>
> Starting in the next chapter, we will stop working with events and switch to commands. Commands are handled in the ViewModel, which makes them easier to test. For now, for convenience, we'll handle events and we'll do so in the code-behind.

Code-behind and event handlers

We see in the Button control listed next that there is a Clicked property that points to a OnCounterClicked method:

```
<Button
  x:Name="CounterBtn"
  Clicked="OnCounterClicked"
  HorizontalOptions="Center"
```

```
SemanticProperties.Hint="Counts the number of times you
   click"
Text="Click me" />
```

This method (`onCounterClicked`) is found in the code-behind file, `MainPage.xaml.cs`. All **event handlers** take two parameters: an object that is the element that raised the event (called the sender), and an object of type `EventArgs` (or a class derived from `EventArgs`). By convention, the `EventArgs` parameter is named `e`.

In our case (and most cases), we don't care about the sender and the simple `EventArgs` (as used here) is empty and serves only as a base class for derived classes that provide additional information to the event handler (thus you might have a type derived from `EventArgs` that provides information that the event handler needs):

```
private void OnCounterClicked(object sender, EventArgs e)
{
    count++;

    if (count == 1)

        CounterBtn.Text = $"Clicked {count} time";
    else

        CounterBtn.Text = $"Clicked {count} times";

    SemanticScreenReader.Announce(CounterBtn.Text);
}
```

The event handler name matches the event handler identified in the XAML.

```
<Button
    Clicked="OnCounterClicked"
```

This handler's job is only to update the text on the button each time the button is clicked. Finally, it uses the `SemanticScreenReader` Announce method to show that text, again for screen readers:

The count instance field is declared at the top of the class:

```
public partial class MainPage : ContentPage
{
```

```
private int count = 0;

public MainPage()
{

    InitializeComponent();
}
```

> **InitializeComponent**
>
> Notice that the constructor calls `InitializeComponent`. This will be true in the code-behind file of every XAML file. It is the job of `InitializeComponent` to initialize all the elements of the page.

When we get to *Chapter 4*, you'll see that we try to minimize the contents of the code-behind file, principally to facilitate the creation of unit tests. At that point, we'll substitute commands for our events, but let's hold off on that for now.

While nearly all the Microsoft documentation and all the existing sample code uses XAML for markup, it is possible to create layouts and views in C#. In fact, in recent years, more and more of the Microsoft documentation shows both.

> **.NET MAUI Community Toolkit**
>
> This section requires the .NET MAUI Community Toolkit that you added as a NuGet package in the previous chapter. The Community Toolkit is actually part of a set of toolkits that are open source projects and supplement what is in the release version of .NET MAUI. They are created by community members who work closely with Microsoft developers. It is fair to assume that many of the Community Toolkit features will migrate into .NET MAUI properly over time. I would strongly urge you to use these toolkits, and this book does so.

If you can do it in XAML, you can do it in C#

Anything that can be declared in XAML can be declared in C#. Containment is managed by using the `children` property of an object. Event handlers must be registered on an instance of the control. That is, an event handler would be registered for a particular button, as you'll see in this example.

Here is the code we wrote in XAML converted to C#:

```
using CommunityToolkit.Maui.Markup;        [1]

namespace ForgetMeNotDemo;

class MainPageCS : ContentPage
{
  private readonly Button counterBtn = new Button   [2]
  {
    Text = "Click Me",
    HorizontalOptions = LayoutOptions.Center,
  }.SemanticHint("Counts the number of times you click");


  public MainPageCS()
  {
    counterBtn.Clicked += OnCounterClicked;     [3]

    Content = new VerticalStackLayout     [4]
    {
      Spacing = 30,
      Padding = new Thickness(30, 0),
      VerticalOptions = LayoutOptions.Center,
      Children =    [5]
              {
                new Image()
                {
                    Source = "dotnet_bot.png",
                    HeightRequest = 200,
                    HorizontalOptions =
                      LayoutOptions.Center,
                }.SemanticDescription("Cute dot net bot
                    waving hi to you!"), [6]

                new Label()
                {
```

```
                        Text="Hello, World",
                        FontSize=32,
                        HorizontalOptions =
                            LayoutOptions.Center,
                    }.SemanticHeadingLevel
                        (SemanticHeadingLevel.Level1),

                    new Label()
                    {
                        Text = "Welcome to .NET Multi-
                            platform App UI",
                        FontSize = 18,
                        HorizontalOptions =
                            LayoutOptions.Center,
                    }.SemanticHeadingLevel
                        (SemanticHeadingLevel.Level2)
                        .SemanticDescription(
                            "Welcome to dot net Multi
                                platform App UI"),

                    counterBtn, [7]
                }
        };
}

private int count = 0;
private void OnCounterClicked(object sender, EventArgs e)
    [8]
{
    count++;

    if (count == 1)
        counterBtn.Text = $"Clicked {count} time";
    else
        counterBtn.Text = $"Clicked {count} times";
```

```
        SemanticScreenReader.Announce(counterBtn.Text);
    }
}
```

Let's quickly take a look at hooking up this new `MainPage`. To test this C# version, set the `ShellContent` element in `AppShell.xaml` to point to your new page like this:

```
<ShellContent
    Title="Home"
    ContentTemplate="{DataTemplate local:MainPageCS}"
    Route="MainPageCS" />
```

Coming back to the XAML converted to C# code, let's break it down for a better understanding. The numbers refer to the numbers in square brackets in the code:

1. We begin by adding a `using` statement for `CommunityToolkit`. We need this for the semantic hints, which are used by screen readers for people with limited or no eyesight. While a finished project should have these for every control, we won't be using them in this book to save space and confusion.

2. We want to add a button, and that button will need an event handler (for the click event). In this example, the event handler for the `Clicked` event is at the bottom of the file. To add an event handler to our button, we must first define `Button`. We do this outside of the constructor and we set its properties [2].

3. At the very beginning of the constructor, we assign the event handler method to the `Clicked` event. As noted, that event handler method is at the bottom of the file, though of course it could be (and perhaps should be) in its own file [3].

4. We are now ready to create `VerticalStackLayout` and all the elements contained within the stack layout [4].

5. These elements will be in the stack layout's `Children` collection [5].

6. Notice that the semantic description is attached to the image using a fluent syntax [6].

7. After all the other elements, we are ready to insert our button into the stack layout's `Children` collection [7].

8. We've put the event handler for the button at the bottom of this file, though you certainly could move it to a different file, probably in a different folder. If you do so, however, remember to add a `using` statement for that namespace [8].

A note on comments

There is a raging controversy in the industry about the use of comments in C# code. I take a rather extreme position: code should be almost completely self-explanatory. That is, if you use appropriate and descriptive names for variables, fields, methods, and so on, no comments should be needed. I'm not a fanatic about this; if the code is sufficiently complex, a comment here and there can be a big help, but comments *rust* and should be used sparingly. Thus, you will find few comments in the code, though we will walk through the code in some detail in the paragraphs that follow each listing.

A recent addition to our tool set is the ability to use Fluent C#, which can make your C# code tighter and yet easier to read.

C# versus Fluent C#

In addition to using C# to create your pages, there is a new (as of Winter 2022) **Community Toolkit** for Fluent C#. This does not change the basic approach but can make creating C# pages cleaner and easier to understand.

To use this, you'll need to add the CommunityToolkit.Maui.Markup NuGet package. Refer to the following figure:

Figure 3.4 – Getting the markup package from NuGet

The project is open source and can be examined (and extended!) at https://github.com/communitytoolkit/Maui.Markup. The ReadMe file will get you started, though we'll cover that material in this book as well.

The first thing you need to do is to update MauiProgram.cs to add the toolkit to the builder using the following code snippet:

```
public static MauiApp CreateMauiApp()
{
    var builder = MauiApp.CreateBuilder();
    builder
        .UseMauiApp<App>()
```

```
    .UseMauiCommunityToolkit()
    .UseMauiCommunityToolkitMarkup()
    .ConfigureFonts(fonts =>
    {
        fonts.AddFont("OpenSans-Regular.ttf",
            "OpenSansRegular");
        fonts.AddFont("OpenSans-Semibold.ttf",
            "OpenSansSemibold");
    });
```

You can and should chain `UseMauiCommunityToolkitMarkup` to `UseMauiCommunityToolkit` in the builder [1].

Now, you can avoid writing this:

```
var entry = new Entry();
entry.WidthRequest = 400;
entry.HeightRequest = 40;
```

Instead, you can chain all of that together and just write this:

```
new Entry().Size(200,40);
```

This makes the code much cleaner.

I will provide C# and Fluent C# examples throughout the book; although, as noted, the primary markup language we'll use is XAML.

Summary

In this chapter, we examined the markup language XAML, which is used to create layouts and controls. We saw that anything that can be done in XAML can also be done in C#, and we saw that there are two ways to write that C#: the traditional declarative way and the newer fluent form.

We examined a few important classes (`Button`, `Label`, `Image`, and so on) and how events can be handled in the code-behind class. I also hinted that code-behind event handlers will be replaced by commands and their implementation in the ViewModel in the next chapter.

In *Chapter 4*, we'll dive into the principal architecture for writing apps in .NET MAUI: **Model-View-ViewModel (MVVM)** and we'll look at data binding. We'll then explore a number of controls and how they can work together.

Quiz

1. In a sentence, what is XAML?

2. What is XAML used for?

3. What is an alternative to using XAML?

4. How do we nest one layout inside another using C#?

5. What is an event handler?

6. If an event is declared in XAML, where is the event handler?

Try it out

Time to start writing code!

Create a new project named `ForgetMeNotJesse` (you might want to use your own name where I have put mine). Ideally, put that project under source control (see the *Technical requirements* section at the top of this chapter).

Use the .NET MAUI template to create your project, using the latest version of .NET (.NET 7 at the time of the writing of this book).

Run your program to make sure everything is set up correctly.

Change `MainPage` so that clicking on the button updates a label below the button with the number of clicks (in addition to displaying it on the button itself).

Once the page is working as intended, create a new page and recreate your `MainPage` in C# rather than in XAML. To test it, remember to set the `ShellContent` element in `AppShell.xaml` to point to your new page like this:

```
<ShellContent
    Title="Home"
    ContentTemplate="{DataTemplate local:MainPageCS}"
    Route="MainPageCS" />
```

If you get stuck at any point, pull down the XAML and C# branch from the book's repository and compare that solution with yours.

4

MVVM and Controls

In *Chapter 3*, we examined the fundamentals of .NET MAUI, but our code was in the code-behind files associated with XAML files. It is time, though, to turn our attention to the consensus architecture for .NET MAUI.

Model-View-ViewModel (**MVVM**) is not a tool or a platform but an architecture. Simply put, it is a way of organizing your code and thinking to optimize the creation of .NET MAUI applications and to facilitate unit testing (see *Chapter 9*).

At its simplest, MVVM consists of three sets of files, that is three namespaces, which essentially means three folders (with subfolders as needed). Taken in turn, `Model` is the set of classes that define the *shape* of your data. This just means that the classes that represent data are held in the model.

`View` is, in simple words, the page that the user sees.

`ViewModel` is where all the action happens. It is the set of classes that manage the logic of your program and that contain the *properties* that are presented in `View`. We'll get into **ViewModel** (**VM**) properties as we go.

In this chapter, we will explore the following topics:

- Setting up MVMM
- Data binding
- Views
- XAML versus C#
- Behaviors
- Popups and dialogs
- Brushes

Technical requirements

For this chapter, you will need the latest version of Visual Studio (any edition).

Each chapter in this book is saved as a branch. The code shown in this chapter and the next is in the branch at `https://github.com/PacktPublishing/.NET-MAUI-for-C-Sharp-Developers/tree/MVVMAndControls`. If you check out the branch you'll see where we ended up, but if you want some of the intermediate steps, just examine the commits that contributed to the branch. To follow along, however, check out the branch at `https://github.com/PacktPublishing/.NET-MAUI-for-C-Sharp-Developers/tree/Navigation/tree/XAMLAndCSharp` as the starting point.

Setting up for MVVM

MVVM is as much a way to organize your files and folders as it is an architectural approach. To get started using MVVM we'll do two things:

1. Create the folders.
2. Download the associated Community Toolkits.

Creating folders

We will be creating three folders. Before I tell you the names of these folders, I should say there is some disagreement about what exactly to name them. *Table 4.1* shows the folder names and their alternatives:

Name we'll use	Alternative 1	Alternative 2
Model	Models	
View	Views	Pages
ViewModel	ViewModels	

Table 4.1 – Naming the folders

As you can see, the key difference is whether or not the name of the folder should use the plural, reflecting the fact that there will be more than one file in each folder, or the singular (as we will do), reflecting the name Model-View-ViewModel. I can't think of a less important controversy, and it clearly doesn't matter what you choose as long as you are consistent. Arbitrarily, we'll use the first.

Thus, create three folders in your project: `Model`, `View`, and `ViewModel`, as shown in *Figure 4.1*:

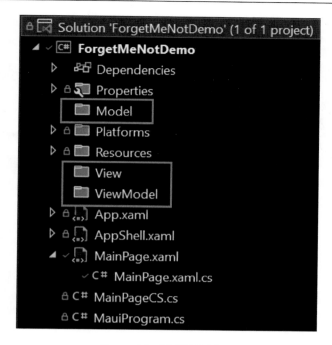

Figure 4.1 – MVVM Folders

MainPage is now in the wrong place. Drag MainPage.xaml to the View folder (it will bring its code-behind with it). You need to fix the namespace in the XAML file:

```
x:Class="ForgetMeNotDemo.View.MainPage"
```

And in the code behind:

```
namespace ForgetMeNotDemo.View;
```

Microsoft provides libraries that are not part of .NET MAUI as they were created by the .NET community, but which, nonetheless, Microsoft endorses and supports. Much of the functionality of these community toolkits will probably migrate into .NET MAUI itself.

The MVVM Community Toolkit

Open **Nuget Manager** (right-click on the solution and choose **Manage NuGet Packages For The Solution,** and click on **Browse**. In the search window enter CommunityToolkit-MVVM and click on **CommunityToolkit.MVVM**. This wonderful toolkit will make programming with MVVM infinitely easier than it otherwise would be. See *Figure 4.2*:

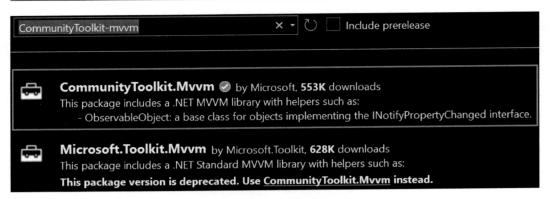

Figure 4.2 – Getting the NuGet package

We'll come back to how to use this toolkit when we talk about *source code generators*. Next, let's take a look at some of the views.

Exploring views

.NET MAUI Controls is a generic term for pages, layouts, and views. In this chapter, we will look at views, while pages and layouts will be reviewed in the next chapter. In *Chapter 7*, we'll look at navigating between pages.

> **Views versus pages**
>
> From the perspective of MVVM, a view is a page. From the perspective of .NET MAUI, View is a control. So, just to keep you totally confused, a View consists of Views and layouts. To avoid this absurdity, we'll refer to the latter as controls. Some frameworks call these widgets. From time to time I'll forget and refer to these controls as Views, but the context will make clear what I mean.

A .NET MAUI Control is an object that maps to native controls on each target platform. Thus, a .NET MAUI Button maps to an iOS, Android, Macintosh, and Windows native Button.

The principal way to display text is with Label. The inheritance tree for Label is as follows:

Object > BindableObject > Element > NavigableElement >

VisualElement > View > Label

An object is, of course, the base for every class in C#. We'll skip over BindableObject for now, and we'll group Element, NavigableElement, and VisualElement together as things you can see on your page. This brings us to View as described previously, and then Label itself.

The most common property to use on Label is Text. Text is what Label displays, thus you can write the following:

```
<Label Text="Hello World" />
```

This creates a Label that displays the iconic greeting. But there is more you can do with Label, as we saw in the previous chapter.

Forget Me Not labels

Let's look at Labels in the context of Forget Me Not. We already have the application, but it is just what we get out of the box. Let's revise this first page to create the initial page for Forget Me Not.

Please click on the - sign next to VerticalStackLayout on MainPage.xaml That will collapse VerticalStackLayout and allow you to delete it all at once, as shown in *Figure 4.3*:

Figure 4.3 – Collapsed VerticalStackLayout

Next, go to the code-behind file (MainPage.xaml.cs) and remove the counter and the OnCounterClicked event handler.

Having cleaned all that out, we are ready to put in new code. We need a layout we can put labels into, so let's create an empty VerticalStackLayout, and add a Label Control to it that says Welcome to Forget Me Not.

```
<VerticalStackLayout>
    <Label Text="Welcome to Forget Me Not"/>
</VerticalStackLayout>
```

We're ready to build on that. Let's add some of the more common properties for making Label look good:

```
<VerticalStackLayout>
    <Label
        x:Name="HelloLabel"
        Margin="20"
        BackgroundColor="Red"
```

```
            FontAttributes="Bold"
            FontSize="Small"
            HorizontalOptions="Center"
            HorizontalTextAlignment="Center"
            Text="Welcome to Forget Me Not"
            TextColor="Yellow"
            VerticalTextAlignment="Center" />
    </VerticalStackLayout>
```

We'll examine each of these properties in turn, but first, *Figure 4.4* shows what the page looks like right now:

Figure 4.4 – Label

Note that the title (**Home**) is an artifact of the page. What we care about is the Label shown below it.

Let's see if we can't make that look a bit nicer before we examine the properties of `Label` by adding just a bit of padding:

```
<VerticalStackLayout>
    <Label
        BackgroundColor="Red"
        FontAttributes="Bold"
        FontSize="Small"
        HorizontalOptions="Center"
        HorizontalTextAlignment="Center"
        LineBreakMode="WordWrap"
        Margin="20"
        MaxLines="5"
        Padding="10"
        Text="Welcome to Forget Me Not"
        TextColor="Yellow"
        VerticalTextAlignment="Center"
```

```
        x:Name="HelloLabel" />
    </VerticalStackLayout>
```

That gives us the page, as shown in *Figure 4.5*.

> **XAML Styler**
>
> Notice that the properties are laid out nicely and in alphabetical order. This is due to a (free) tool named XAML Styler which you can get from the Visual Studio Marketplace (`https://bit.ly/XAMLstyler`).

Figure 4.5 – Label with Padding

Much better. Let's examine the preceding code with the padding line by line.

Most of these properties are self-explanatory. The `BackgroundColor` property controls the entire label. In our case, we've set the `Padding` property (as described in *Chapter 3*) to `10`; thus, the red shows with a padding of `10` all around the text.

As you can see, we set the text to `Bold` using the `FontAttributes` property. The possible attributes are `Bold`, `Italic`, and `None`, with `None` being the default.

`FontSize` can be entered in device-independent units (for example, `FontSize = "20"`) or in one of the enumerated constants such as `Micro`, `Small`, `Large`, and so on.

`HorizontalOptions` and `VerticalOptions` place the label on the page relative to the edges of the page. We touched on this in the previous chapter. In the case of `HorizontalOptions`, the choices are `Start` (far left), `Center` (middle), or `End` (far right).

The next property is `LineBreakMode`, which goes with the `MaxLines` property. Together they determine how many lines of text the label can support and where the lines will be wrapped. To see this, modify the text to say "*Welcome to Forget Me Not, so glad you are here, we couldn't do this without you and we appreciate your patience.*" As you can see in *Figure 4.6*, the text is now centered on multiple lines, and each line breaks at a word boundary.

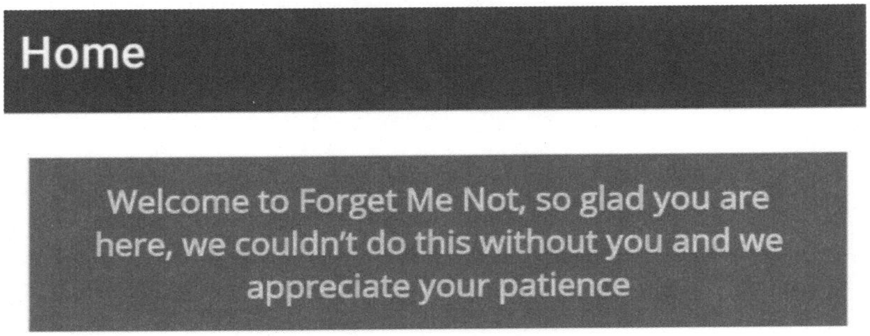

Figure 4.6 – Multi-line Label

As noted earlier, `Label` has dozens of properties, and while we've covered the most important ones, you can always look up the others on Microsoft Learn. In this case, the page you'll need is `https://bit.ly/MicrosoftLabel`.

The key to displaying data in the MVVM model is data binding, which allows us to associate a view and a property and then allows .NET MAUI to keep the view up to date as the value of the property changes. Let's explore this next.

Data binding

One of the most powerful aspects of .NET MAUI is **data binding** and data binding works extremely well with MVVM. The idea is to *bind* data (values) to controls. For example, we might have a class with the text we want to display on this label held on a public property (you can only bind to public properties). Rather than having to copy that text from the class to the label, we just tell the label the name of the property.

The public property will be kept in a class in `ViewModel`. But we have to answer the question how does `View` know where to look for the property? That is handled by setting `BindingContext`.

Let's look at a simple example. In `ViewModel`, create a new file named `MainViewModel.cs`.

> **Naming ViewModel**
>
> The most common naming convention is to name the page with the word page, such as `MainPage` or `LoginPage` but to drop the word page in the `ViewModel` name, such as `MainViewModel` and `LoginViewModel`. So, that is what we'll do in this book.
>
> Note that other programmers will use the `MainPageViewModel` name. On the other hand, some do not use the word *page* but rather *view*, as in `MainView` and `LoginView`. What is most important is for you (and your team) to be consistent so that it is easy to guess and find the associated pages and view models.

Before going ahead, notice that Visual Studio has put your class into the `ForgetMeNotDemo.ViewModel` namespace (if you named your project `ForgetMeNot`, the namespace will be `ForgetMeNot.ViewModel`). This is based on the folder the `.cs` file is in.

Make sure the class is public and that it is marked `partial`. All binding in .NET MAUI is done with partial classes, allowing the rest of the class to be handled internally and by generated partial classes.

Creating a public property

We now want to create a property named `FullName`.

The original way to do this looked something like this:

```
private string fullName;
public string FullName
{
    get => fullName;
    set
    {
        fullName = value;
        OnPropertyChanged();
    }
}
```

However, the absolute best approach is to take advantage of the code generators in the NuGet package we just added. These work by using attributes. Add an attribute above the `[ObservableObject]` class declaration like this:

```
using CommunityToolkit.Mvvm.ComponentModel;
namespace ForgetMeNotDemo.ViewModel;


[ObservableObject]
public partial class MainViewModel
{
}
```

That attribute will allow you to generate properties. Above each property, use the `Observable-Property` attribute:

```
[ObservableProperty]
  private string fullName;
```

This will cause the `NuGet` package to (invisibly) generate the uppercase public property and its `OnPropertyChanged()` method call as if you had entered them yourself.

Before we look at how to set the `FullName` value, we need to set up `BindingContext`.

Setting up BindingContext

`BindingContext` tells your `View` where to get its bound data. You can set this in a number of ways; the most common is to set it in the code-behind file for the `View` class (in this case, `MainPage.xaml.cs`). First, we declare an instance of `ViewModel`:

```
private MainViewModel vm = new MainViewModel();
Next, we assign the BindingContext to that instance in the
  constructor:
public MainPage()
{
  InitializeComponent();
  BindingContext = vm;
}
```

Here is the code behind the class:

```
public partial class MainPage : ContentPage
{

  private MainViewModel vm = new MainViewModel();

  public MainPage()
  {
    InitializeComponent();
    BindingContext = vm;
  }
}
```

Next, we'll see how to assign values to the `ViewModel` class properties.

> **Names**
>
> I don't usually like abbreviations for names. There are rare exceptions, and using vm for `ViewModel` is such a strong convention that I yield to peer-group pressure.

Assigning values to the View Model class properties

You can assign your string in `ViewModel`, in the `ViewModel` constructor, or in the override for the `OnAppearing` method. `OnAppearing` is called before `View` is displayed and looks like this (you put this in the code-behind file):

```
protected override void OnAppearing()
{
  base.OnAppearing();
  vm.FullName = "Jesse Liberty";
}
```

We will return to `OnAppearing` and its sibling `OnDisappearing` method, in *Chapter 7*.

> **InitializeComponent**
>
> `InitializeComponent` must be in the constructor of every code-behind file. It is the responsibility of `InitializeComponent` to initialize all the controls on the page.

Implementing Binding

You are now ready to bind the `FullName` property to `Label`. In the XAML, change the `Label` text property to this:

```
Text="{Binding FullName}"
```

> **Naming properties and fields**
>
> There is a general consensus that properties should be named using Pascal case (as shown in the preceding snippet) and that member fields should be named using camel case (the first letter is lowercase, as in myMemberField), though there is no agreement at all as to whether member fields should be prepended with an underbar as in _myMemberField. We won't use the underbar in this book, but feel free to do so as long, again, as you are consistent.

Using the binding keyword tells Label to get its value from the FullName property found in the ViewModel set by BindingContext.

You will want to pay attention to the syntax. It is always as shown here: open quotes, open braces, the Binding keyword, property name, closing brace, and closing quotes. Okay, I lied. It is sometimes more complex, but these elements are always there.

The result of this construct is that the value of FullName is placed inside the Text property of the label, as shown in *Figure 4.7*:

Figure 4.7 – A label with data-bound text

One of the distinguishing characteristics of an MVVM program is that the logic is in ViewModel rather than in the code-behind file, which we will explore next.

ViewModel versus code-behind

The more you can put into ViewModel (rather than the code-behind file) the easier it will be to test your program (see *Chapter 9* on unit testing). Some MVVM fans think *nothing* should be in the code-behind file besides the required call to InitializeComponent. They argue that even setting ViewModel should be done in the XAML to keep the code-behind file as empty as possible.

I take a more moderate view of this. I often set BindingContext in the code-behind file. I do move all my *event handling* out of the code-behind file as you'll see when we talk about commands:

```
LoginPage.xaml.cs:

public partial class LoginPage : ContentPage
{

    LoginViewModel vm = new LoginViewModel();

    public LoginPage()

    {
```

```
        BindingContext = vm;

        InitializeComponent();

    }

}
```

Notice that `BindingContext` here is set before calling `InitializeComponent`. While either can come first in most cases, setting up all your bindings before initializing the page is generally good practice. Thus, we'll stick with the approach shown here.

> **Renegade code-behind**
>
> There are times when it is just much easier to put a method in the code-behind file. Be careful with this, however. 99% of the time, when it seems really important to put something in the code-behind file, you actually can make it work in `ViewModel`, and that is much better (again, for testing). But if you do have to put something in the code-behind file, do not feel bad, and do not let other .NET MAUI programmers push you around.

The center of developing most apps, the part that people respond to, is the **user interface (UI)**. In .NET MAUI, the UI consists of views in layouts. Let's turn our attention to the most important views.

Views

There are many controls for displaying and obtaining data from the user. The following sections will cover the most common and useful ones, including those shown here:

- Images
- Labels
- Buttons
- ImageButtons
- Entering text

Images

You *can* write a .NET MAUI program without images, but it is likely to look pretty boring. Managing images is much easier in .NET MAUI than it was in Xamarin.Forms. Now, instead of having to have one image for each resolution in iOS and Android, you place one image in the resources folder, and .NET MAUI takes care of the rest for all the platforms!

In this example, we'll use an image named flower.png, which you can download from our GitHub repository. If you prefer, though, you can use any image you like. We'll place the image in the Resources > Images folder.

When we are ready to display it, we'll use an **Image View**. Here is a simple example:

```
<Image
    HeightRequest="200"
    HorizontalOptions="Center"
    Source="{Binding FavoriteFlower}" />
```

I've only set three properties, but they accomplish quite a bit. HeightRequest sets, as you might guess, the height of the image on the page in device-independent units (in this case, 200). I've set it to be centered. Most importantly, I've identified the source—that is the name of the image. But rather than lock in the name of the image in View, I've bound it to a property in MainPageViewModel.

The result is that MainPage now looks like *Figure 4.8*:

Figure 4.8 – Binding the source to a property in ViewModel

Of course, there are a number of additional properties you can set. A set of favorites for me are the Rotation properties, which can rotate on the *x*, *y*, and *z* axes. If I add the RotationX property like this:

```
<Image
    HeightRequest="200"
    HorizontalOptions="Center"
    RotationX="45"
    Source="flower.png" />
```

The image rotates, as shown in *Figure 4.9*:

Figure 4.9 – RotationX="45"

Another useful trick is to make the image semi-transparent by setting Opacity to a value between 0 and 1. *Figure 4.10* shows the same image with an opacity of .25. I removed StackLayout and substituted a Grid. More about grids in the next chapter, but if you just declare one and put Label and Image into it with no other Grid properties, they lay one on top of the other:

```
<Grid>
    <Label
        BackgroundColor="Red"
        FontAttributes="Bold"
```

```
            FontSize="Small"
            HeightRequest="50"
            HorizontalOptions="Center"
            HorizontalTextAlignment="Center"
            LineBreakMode="WordWrap"
            Margin="20"
            MaxLines="5"
            Padding="10"
            Text="{Binding FullName}"
            TextColor="Yellow"
            VerticalTextAlignment="Center"
            x:Name="HelloLabel" />

    <Image
            HeightRequest="200"
            HorizontalOptions="Center"
            IsVisible="True"
            Opacity=".25"
            RotationX="45"
            Source="{Binding FavoriteFlower}"
            x:Name="BigFlower" />
</Grid>
```

Figure 4.10 shows the result:

Figure 4.10 – Overlay and semi-transparent effect

There is endless room for creativity.

Clicking on an image

One of the key things that many people want to do with an image is click on it. There are two solutions to this problem. The easiest is to use a button.

Buttons can have text and a number of other properties, but the most important is the command. The command tells `ViewModel` what to do when the button is clicked.

To show how this works, I'm going to put a new property on our image, `IsVisible`, and set it to `true`. As long as that is `true`, the image is visible. But, as you can imagine, setting it false makes the big flower invisible. Not only is it invisible, but it also takes up no space on the page, so the button will be directly under the label.

Here is the code for `Button`:

```
<Button
    Text="Click me"
    Command="{Binding ToggleFlowerVisibilityCommand}"/>
```

This is the simplest button I can make (we'll look at making it nicer in just a bit). The key here is the `Command` parameter. You can tell by the `Binding` keyword that `ToggleFlowerVisibility` will be in `ViewModel`. Sure enough, it is, but rather than declaring a command and pointing it at a method, we can use the code generator to do the heavy lifting for us.

Here is the modified `MainViewModel`:

```
[ObservableObject]
public partial class MainViewModel
{
  [ObservableProperty] private bool flowerIsVisible = true;
    [1]


  [ObservableProperty] private string fullName;
  [ObservableProperty] private string favoriteFlower =
    "flower.png";

  [RelayCommand]    [2]
  private void ToggleFlowerVisibility()    [3]
  {
    FlowerIsVisible = !FlowerIsVisible;
```

```
    }
  }
```

This is an example of *convention over configuration* – the Command property in Button is ToggleFlowerVisibilityCommand, but when you implement it in RelayCommand [2], you name it ToggleFlowerVisibility [3] leaving off Command.

Note that we created FlowerIsVisible [1] as an ObservableProperty, we simply toggle it from true to false and back on each click.

Button properties

As it is now, the button will be displayed as it would appear natively on each platform. But these buttons can be pretty ugly. We can make them much nicer by taking over more of their appearance.

Here is my XAML for Button, which while not beautiful, will illustrate some of the properties you can use to take control of the button's appearance:

```
<Button
    BackgroundColor="Red"
    BorderColor="Black"
    BorderWidth="2"
    Command="{Binding ToggleFlowerVisibilityCommand}"
    CornerRadius="20"
    FontSize="Small"
    HeightRequest="35"
    Padding="5"
    Text="Don't Click Me"
    TextColor="Yellow"
    WidthRequest="150" />
```

There are three new properties that we've not seen before. The first is BorderColor, which goes along with BorderWidth. This provides a border around the button. Since we've set BackgroundColor to Red, the border will stand out. The final new property is CornerRadius, which gives us a nice rounding of the corners of the otherwise square button. Put that all together, and you get a button that looks like *Figure 4.11*:

Figure 4.11 – A nicer-looking button

> **Why is this button still ugly?**
>
> I am certainly not a UI person, and so my pages tend to be fairly ugly until fixed by someone who knows what they are doing. The screen images in this book will reflect that inability.

ImageButton

At times, rather than having text, we'd rather have an image on the button. There is an `ImageButton` control that combines many of the properties of the `Image` control and the `Button` control:

```
<ImageButton
    BorderColor="Black"
    BorderWidth="2"
    Command="{Binding ToggleFlowerVisibilityCommand}"
    MaximumHeightRequest="75"
    MaximumWidthRequest="75"
    Padding="5"
    Source="{Binding FavoriteFlower}" />
```

You can see how similar it is to the `Button` control. In fact, I've preserved the command binding and the source binding, so we end up with a small image of the flower under the big image, but clicking on the small one (`ImageButton`) causes the big one (`Image`) to become invisible and then visible, and so on. I'll show both visible in *Figure 4.12* because it is hard to toggle an image on paper:

Figure 4.12 – ImageButton

TapGestureRecognizer

The second way to handle tapping on an image is to assign a gesture recognizer. The type of `GestureRecognizer` we're going to assign is `TapGestureRecognizer`, which will recognize when the image itself has been tapped. To be safe, we'll set it so that the image has to be double-tapped. When that happens, the image will "poof!" disappear.

We'll remove `ImageButton`, and just have `Image` (and `Label`). Here is our new XAML file:

```xml
<?xml version="1.0" encoding="utf-8" ?>
<ContentPage
    BackgroundColor="White"
    x:Class="ForgetMeNotDemo.View.MainPage"
    xmlns="http://schemas.microsoft.com/dotnet/2021/maui"
    xmlns:x="http://schemas.microsoft.com/winfx/2009/xaml">

    <ScrollView>
        <VerticalStackLayout>
            <Label
                BackgroundColor="Red"
                FontAttributes="Bold"
                FontSize="Small"
                HeightRequest="50"
                HorizontalOptions="Center"
                HorizontalTextAlignment="Center"
                LineBreakMode="WordWrap"
                Margin="20"
                MaxLines="5"
                Padding="10"
                Text="{Binding FullName}"
                TextColor="Yellow"
                VerticalTextAlignment="Center"
                x:Name="HelloLabel" />

            <Image
                HeightRequest="200"
                HorizontalOptions="Center"
                IsVisible="{Binding FlowerIsVisible}" [1]
```

```
          Source="{Binding FavoriteFlower}"
          x:Name="BigFlower">
          <Image.GestureRecognizers>         [2]
              <TapGestureRecognizer          [3]
                  Command="{Binding
                      ImageTappedCommand}"    [4]
                  NumberOfTapsRequired="2" /> [5]
          </Image.GestureRecognizers>
        </Image>
      </VerticalStackLayout>
    </ScrollView>

</ContentPage>
```

We see at [1] that the image starts as visible. Between the opening and closing brackets for Image we add GestureRecognizer [2]. Within GestureRecognizer we add TapGestureRecognizer [3], and we define ImageTappedCommand [4] just as we did with other commands. Finally, we declare that for the command to fire, the user must tap twice [5].

Here is an example of RelayCommand from ViewModel:

```
[RelayCommand]
private void ImageTapped()
{
  FlowerIsVisible = !FlowerIsVisible;
}
```

As you can see, this handler is nearly identical to the previous one. However, this one won't work as intended. Before reading further, try to figure out what will happen when we double-click on the image (to make it invisible) and then try to do so again (to make it visible). Take your time. I'll wait here.

You can solve this by going back to Button, or perhaps putting a GestureRcognizer on the Label.

When you double-tap on the image, it does, in fact, disappear because IsVisible is set to false. However, once it disappears, it is gone, and there is nothing there to tap on to bring it back:

```
<Label
    BackgroundColor="Red"
    FontAttributes="Bold"
    FontSize="Small"
    HeightRequest="50"
```

```
        HorizontalOptions="Center"
        HorizontalTextAlignment="Center"
        LineBreakMode="WordWrap"
        Margin="20"
        MaxLines="5"
        Padding="10"
        Text="{Binding FullName}"
        TextColor="Yellow"
        VerticalTextAlignment="Center"
        x:Name="HelloLabel">
        <Label.GestureRecognizers>
            <TapGestureRecognizer Command="{Binding
                ImageTappedCommand}" />
        </Label.GestureRecognizers>
    </Label>
```

What's interesting here is that the `TapGestureRecognizer` command points to the same `RelayCommand`; it will be invoked either by double-tapping on the image or single-tapping on the label.

The following are two takeaway points from this section:

- `TapGestureRecognizer` allows you to make any control tappable, which can be pretty powerful.
- Once `View` is invisible, it is no longer on the page. You can make it visible again from the code behind, but only if you do so by way of a different control (as we did with `ButtonImage`).

After displaying text, the most important aspect of an app is the ability to obtain text from the user. For that, the principal views are `Entry` and `Editor`. Let's have a look at them next.

Entering text

We've looked at displaying text, let's turn our attention to entering text. There are two controls that are principally responsible for this:

1. `Entry`: Used for entering a line of text
2. `Editor`: Used for entering multiple lines of text

These two controls are obviously related, but they have different properties. `Entry` is designed to take a single line of text and `Editor` handles multi-line entry.

To see these views at work, let's create a login page for Forget Me Not.

Forget Me Not login page

We've been playing with the `MainPage`, but in truth, the actual application has a very simple `MainPage`: just the image. Things get more interesting with the login page. We will make a first approximation of the login page as it will allow us to use the `Entry` and `Editor` controls, though we will evolve this page as we go.

Creating the login page

The first task is to create the login page. To do so, right-click on the **View** folder, and choose **Add Item**. In the dialog box click on **.NET MAUI** in the left pane, and on **.NET MAUI ContentPage (XAML)** on the right. Name the page `LoginPage.xaml`, as shown in *Figure 4.13*:

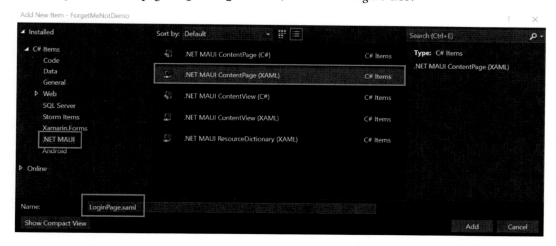

Figure 4.13 – Add Item dialog box

XAML versus C#

If you wish to create the UI for the login page using C# rather than XAML, choose **ContentPage (C#)** instead. We'll look at both in this section, but let's start with the XAML version.

Examine the XAML page out of the box. The class is set to `ForgetMeNotDemo.View.LoginPage`, reflecting the namespace (when we created the file under `View` that became the namespace automatically). The XAML also has `VerticalStackLayout` and inside that, `Label`.

Take a very quick look at the code-behind file. Note that `namespace` has been created for you and that the page derives from `ContentPage`.

Go back to the XAML page and delete `Label` in `VerticalScrollView`. When the application is complete, it should look like *Figure 4.14*:

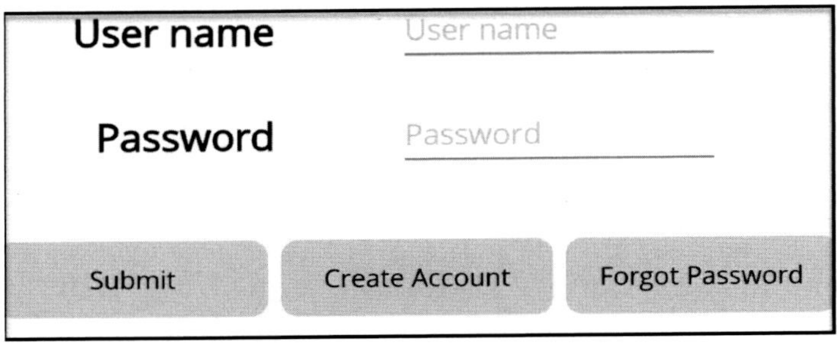

Figure 4.14 – Login.XAML (top portion)

As you can see, we have two labels. To the right of each label is an entry, and the entry has placeholder text. As soon as you start typing in the entry, the placeholder text will disappear.

There are also three buttons. To lay this out properly, we'd like to use Grid, but we're not covering grids until *Chapter 6*, *Layouts*. That's not a problem, though, because it gives us the opportunity to look at nesting StackLayouts and using HorizontalStackLayout.

To get started, we'll just create the top line. We'd like flexibility for the text in the label, and we'd like to capture the *User name* entry in a property of ViewModel that we haven't created yet. Let's do that now. Right-click on the **ViewModel** folder and create a new LoginViewModel class.

In LoginViewModel add ObservableProperty for the user name:

```
namespace ForgetMeNotDemo.ViewModel
{
    [ObservableObject]
    internal partial class LoginViewModel
    {
        [ObservableProperty] private string name;
```

When the user types a name into the Entry control it will be saved in this property.

> **OneWay and TwoWay binding**
> Controls can be OneWay, in which case the control gets its value from the data source (in this case, the property) but can't send it back, or TwoWay, in which case the control gets its data from the data source but can also write a value back. Entry defaults to TwoWay.

We're ready to create the top line in LoginPage in XAML:

```
<?xml version="1.0" encoding="utf-8" ?>
<ContentPage
```

```
    Title="LoginPage"
    x:Class="ForgetMeNotDemo.View.LoginPage"
    xmlns="http://schemas.microsoft.com/dotnet/2021/maui"
    xmlns:x="http://schemas.microsoft.com/winfx/2009/xaml">
    <VerticalStackLayout>
        <HorizontalStackLayout WidthRequest="300">
            <Label
                FontSize="Medium"
                HorizontalOptions="Start"
                Margin="10,20,10,0"
                Text="User Name"
                VerticalOptions="Center"
                VerticalTextAlignment="Center" />
            <Entry
                HorizontalOptions="End"
                Placeholder="User Name"
                Text="{Binding Name}"
                WidthRequest="150" />
        </HorizontalStackLayout>
    </VerticalStackLayout>
</ContentPage>
```

We're using three properties on Entry:

1. HorizontalOptions: Here we are setting it to End so that Entry will be to the far right of the line

2. PlaceHolder: This is the text that will be displayed until the user starts to enter text

3. Text: We have bound this to the Name property in ViewModel

There is one problem looking at this page: there is no way to get there (yet). For now, rather than having the program open at MainPage, we'll have it open to our new LoginPage. To do so, go to AppShell.xaml and change ShellContent to look like this:

```
<ShellContent
    Title="Home"
    ContentTemplate="{DataTemplate view1:LoginPage}"
    Route="LoginPage" />
```

We'll be discussing the Shell and routing in *Chapter 7*, but this will work for now.

Run the program. If you run it on an Android device or emulator, it should look more or less like *Figure 4.15*:

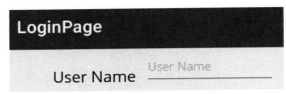

Figure 4.15 – LoginPage, the first iteration

Even for me, it's not very attractive, but it does demonstrate the controls and the layout. Try typing in the **User Name** entry. Notice that the placeholder text disappears instantly.

We need a way to tell whether the value you entered is really binding to the Name property. To do this, let's add a label and bind it to the Name property. That way, when we enter text into the entry it will be reflected in Label:

```xml
<?xml version="1.0" encoding="utf-8" ?>
<ContentPage
    Title="LoginPage"
    x:Class="ForgetMeNotDemo.View.LoginPage"
    xmlns="http://schemas.microsoft.com/dotnet/2021/maui"
    xmlns:x="http://schemas.microsoft.com/winfx/2009/xaml">
    <VerticalStackLayout>
        <HorizontalStackLayout WidthRequest="300">
            <Label
                FontSize="Medium"
                HorizontalOptions="Start"
                Margin="10,20,10,0"
                Text="User Name"
                VerticalOptions="Center"
                VerticalTextAlignment="Center" />
            <Entry
                HorizontalOptions="End"
                Placeholder="User Name"
                Text="{Binding Name}"
                WidthRequest="150" />
```

```
        </HorizontalStackLayout>
        <Label
            Margin="10,30,10,0"
            Text="{Binding Name}" />
    </VerticalStackLayout>
</ContentPage>
```

However, before we can make that work, we have to set up BindingContext, as we did on MainPage. Open the code-behind file for the XAML page and set up LoginViewModel as the binding context:

```
public partial class LoginPage : ContentPage
{

    LoginViewModel vm = new LoginViewModel();

public LoginPage()

    {


        BindingContext = vm;


        InitializeComponent();


    }

}
```

When we run this and type into the entry the text is saved in the Name property in ViewModel. Since the label is bound to the same property, the text is immediately shown there as well, as seen in *Figure 4.16*:

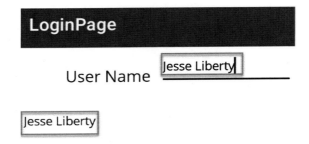

Figure 4.16 – Proving that the entry is binding to the Name property

Now that we know it is working, delete the label. Let's do the same thing for the password that we did for the name, except that we don't want anyone to see the password we're entering. No problem, Entry has a boolean property, IsPassword, which we'll set to True:

```xml
<?xml version="1.0" encoding="utf-8" ?>
<ContentPage
    Title="LoginPage"
    x:Class="ForgetMeNotDemo.View.LoginPage"
    xmlns="http://schemas.microsoft.com/dotnet/2021/maui"
    xmlns:x="http://schemas.microsoft.com/winfx/2009/xaml">
    <VerticalStackLayout>
        <HorizontalStackLayout WidthRequest="300">
            <Label
                FontSize="Medium"
                HorizontalOptions="Start"
                Margin="10,20,10,0"
                Text="User Name"
                VerticalOptions="Center"
                VerticalTextAlignment="Center" />
            <Entry
                HorizontalOptions="End"
                Placeholder="User Name"
                Text="{Binding Name}"
                WidthRequest="150" />
        </HorizontalStackLayout>
        <HorizontalStackLayout WidthRequest="300">
            <Label
                FontSize="Medium"
```

```
                     HorizontalOptions="Start"
                     Margin="10,10,10,0"
                     Text="Password"
                     VerticalOptions="Center"
                     VerticalTextAlignment="Center" />
             <Entry
                     HorizontalOptions="End"
                     Placeholder="Password"
                     IsPassword="True"
                     Text="{Binding Password}"
                     WidthRequest="150" />
        </HorizontalStackLayout>


    </VerticalStackLayout>
</ContentPage>
```

Before continuing, notice that we have VerticalStackLayout that contains two HorizontalStackLayouts. This is a not uncommon layout, but again we'll get more control over the appearance when we move on to Grid.

The result of this XAML is shown in *Figure 4.17*:

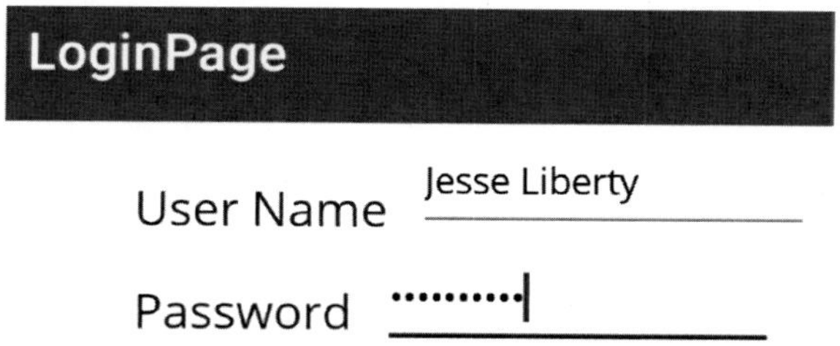

Figure 4.17 – Using the password Boolean on Entry

Let's complete this first iteration of the page by adding the three buttons. We'll only give one (**Submit**) a command for now:

```
<HorizontalStackLayout Margin="10,10,10,0">
    <Button
        BackgroundColor="Gray"
        Command="{Binding SubmitCommand}"
        Margin="5"
```

```
            Text="Submit" />
    <Button
        BackgroundColor="Gray"
        Margin="5"
        Text="Create Account" />
    <Button
        BackgroundColor="Gray"
        Margin="5"
        Text="Forgot Password" />
</HorizontalStackLayout>
```

The result is shown in *Figure 4.18*:

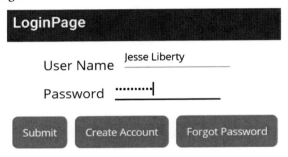

Figure 4.18 – Adding the buttons

When you run this, you may notice that it works fine, except that clicking on **Submit** doesn't do anything. That is because we named the command but never implemented it. We're going to save doing so for a while. Actually, for a long while. We'll tackle the real implementation when we get to *Chapter 11, Working with the API*.

The Title

You may have noticed that the page has a **LoginPage** title. The good news is that we got that for free (.NET MAUI created it when we created the page). However, it would be nice to have a space between **Login** and **Page**.

At the top of the XAML page is the declaration of ContentPage, and the first property set there is Title.

```
<ContentPage
    Title="LoginPage"
```

Just insert the missing space, and all will be right with the world.

Editor

The second primary way of entering text into your application is with the `Editor` control. The principal difference from the `Entry` class is that `Editor` is designed for multi-line data entry. You have a lot of control over the text, as you'll see in the next example.

Let's add an editor to the login page. We'll set it so that it is only visible if the user clicks on **Forgot Password**. The user will be encouraged to explain exactly where the password was the last time they saw it and why they were so careless when we told them to keep the password secure.

Reopen `LoginPage.xaml` and add an `Editor` inside `VerticalStackLayout`, at the very bottom:

```
<Editor
    FontSize="Small"
    HeightRequest="300"
    IsTextPredictionEnabled="True"   [1]
    Margin="10"
    MaxLength="500"    [2]
    Placeholder="Explain yourself here (up to 500
      characters)"
    PlaceholderColor="Red" [3]
    Text="{Binding LostPasswordExcuse}"
    TextColor="Blue"    [4]
    VerticalTextAlignment="Center" [5]
    x:Name="LoginEditor" />
```

I've used a number of properties on the editor, and a few of them are new.

[1] `IsTextPredictionEnabled` allows your editor to offer the user text to complete their sentence. You've seen this, no doubt, when working with Gmail and other applications. This is actually `True` by default; you might want to set it to `False` when asking for a user's name or other conditions in which the prediction might be annoying.

[2] `MaxLength` manages how many characters the user may enter into the editor.

[3] `PlaceHolderColor` allows you to set the color of the placeholder text.

[4] Similarly, `TextColor` sets the color of the text the user enters.

[5] `VerticalTextAlignment` sets where, within the editor, the text will lie.

Figure 4.19 shows what **Login Page** looks like before the user enters anything into the editor, and *Figure 4.20* shows what it looks like after the user has entered a few lines of text:

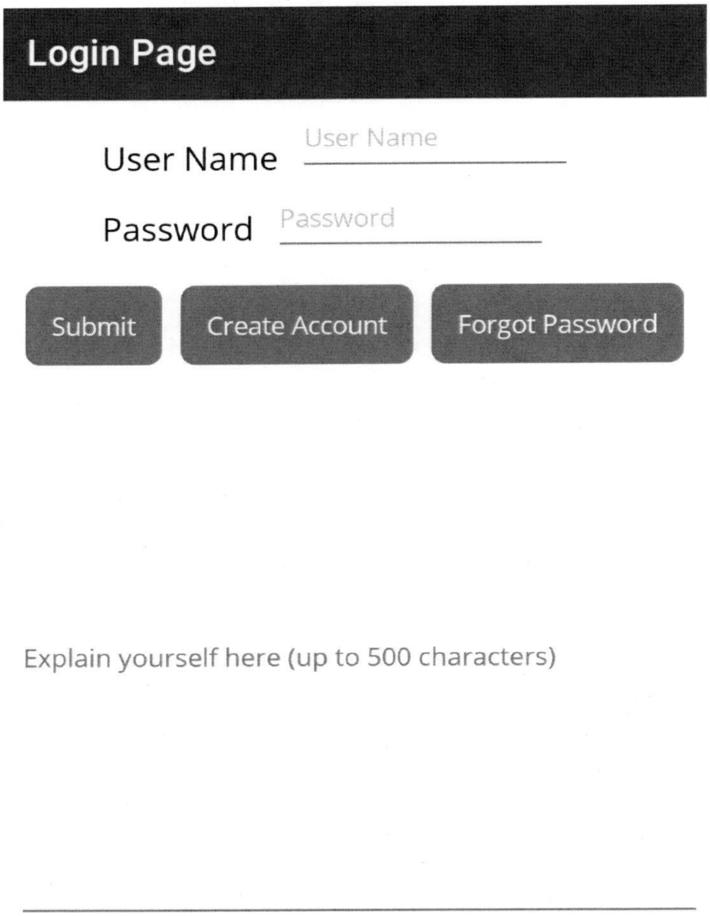

Figure 4.19 – Before the user enters text into the editor

You can enter as much text as you want into the editor, up to whatever maximum you've set in the declaration of the control.

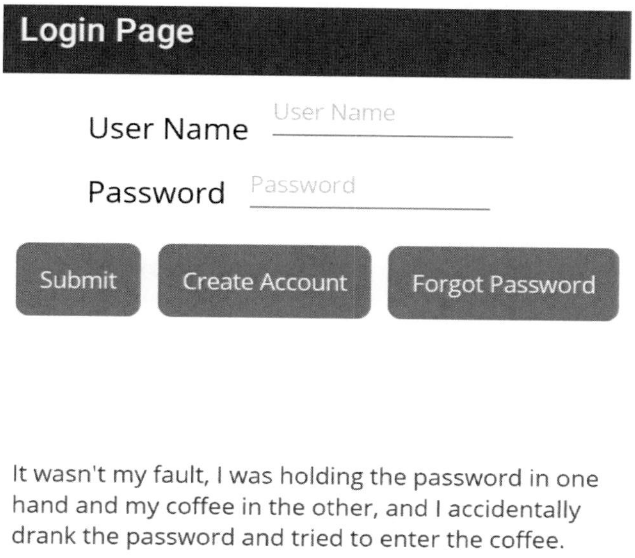

Figure 4.20 – After the user enters text into the editor

Although the margin is only set to 10, there is a huge space between the buttons and the text. That is because we set VerticalTextAlignment to Center. If we change it to Start, the text will move to the top of the editor, as shown in *Figure 4.21*:

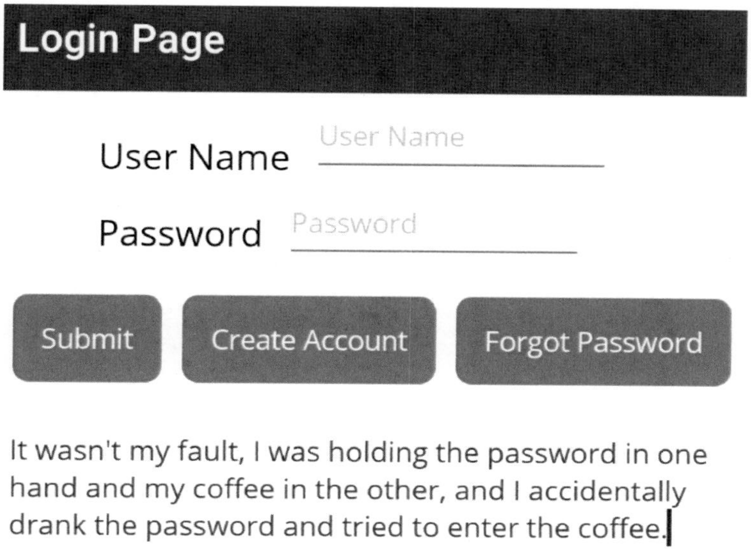

Figure 4.21 – Moving the text in the editor to the top (start) position

Buttons inherently rely on events, but events are handled in the code-behind file, and we'd like to keep all our logic in `ViewModel`. The answer to that is the `EventToCommand` behavior, which we will consider next.

Behaviors

The `Editor` control has a number of events. These can be handled by event handlers in the code-behind file, but for the reasons already explained (and explained) we'd rather not do that. So, here enters behaviors.

Behaviors let you add functionality to your controls without having to create subclasses. They *tack on* the behavior. What we want to do now is tack on the ability to manage commands in a control (`Editor`) that doesn't have commands.

The .NET MAUI Community Toolkit comes with a plethora of behaviors, including `EventToCommandBehavior`. This wonderful behavior allows you to transform an event (which would be handled in the code-behind file) into a command, which can be handled in `ViewModel`.

The event we want to change in `Editor` is `OnEditorCompleted`, which is raised when the user hits the *Enter* key (or, on Windows, the *Tab* key):

```
<Editor
    FontSize="Small"
    HeightRequest="300"
    IsTextPredictionEnabled="True"
    Margin="10"
    MaxLength="500"
    Placeholder="Explain yourself here (up to 500
        characters)"
    PlaceholderColor="Red"
    Text="{Binding LostPasswordExcuse}"
    TextColor="Blue"
    VerticalTextAlignment="Start"
    x:Name="LoginEditor">
    <Editor.Behaviors>
        <behaviors:EventToCommandBehavior
            EventName="Completed"
            Command="{Binding EditorCompletedCommand}" />
    </Editor.Behaviors>
</Editor>
```

The syntax is reminiscent of GestureRecognizers, and that is not a coincidence. The idea is to enable a control to have various collections and to be able to declare those collections in the XAML.

You can, of course, declare the same thing in C#:

```
Var editor = new Editor();


var behavior = new EventToCommandBehavior
{
    EventName = nameof(Editor.Completed),
    Command= new EditorCompletedCommand()
};
```

As noted earlier, anything you can do in XAML, you can also do in C#.

You manage the command (however you create it) in ViewModel, just as you would any other command. For fun, let's add a label below the editor and bind it to LostPasswordExcuse, but only show it until the user presses *Enter*.

Login.xaml now looks like this:

```
<?xml version="1.0" encoding="utf-8" ?>
<ContentPage
    Title="Login Page"
    x:Class="ForgetMeNotDemo.View.LoginPage"
    xmlns="http://schemas.microsoft.com/dotnet/2021/maui"
    xmlns:behaviors="http://schemas.microsoft.com/dotnet/
        2022/maui/toolkit"
    xmlns:x="http://schemas.microsoft.com/winfx/2009/xaml">
    <VerticalStackLayout>
        <HorizontalStackLayout WidthRequest="300">
            <Label
                FontSize="Medium"
                HorizontalOptions="Start"
                Margin="10,20,10,0"
                Text="User Name"
                VerticalOptions="Center"
                VerticalTextAlignment="Center" />
            <Entry
                HorizontalOptions="End"
```

```
            Placeholder="User Name"
            Text="{Binding Name}"
            WidthRequest="150" />
    </HorizontalStackLayout>
    <HorizontalStackLayout WidthRequest="300">
        <Label
            FontSize="Medium"
            HorizontalOptions="Start"
            Margin="10,10,10,0"
            Text="Password"
            VerticalOptions="Center"
            VerticalTextAlignment="Center" />
        <Entry
            HorizontalOptions="End"
            IsPassword="True"
            Placeholder="Password"
            Text="{Binding Password}"
            WidthRequest="150" />
    </HorizontalStackLayout>
    <HorizontalStackLayout Margin="10,10,10,0">
        <Button
            BackgroundColor="Gray"
            Command="{Binding SubmitCommand}"
            Margin="5"
            Text="Submit" />
        <Button
            BackgroundColor="Gray"
            Margin="5"
            Text="Create Account" />
        <Button
            BackgroundColor="Gray"
            Margin="5"
            Text="Forgot Password" />
    </HorizontalStackLayout>
    <Editor
        FontSize="Small"
```

```
            HeightRequest="300"
            IsTextPredictionEnabled="True"
            Margin="10"
            MaxLength="5"
            Placeholder="Explain yourself here (up to 500
                characters)"
            PlaceholderColor="Red"
            Text="{Binding LostPasswordExcuse}"
            TextColor="Blue"
            VerticalTextAlignment="Start"
            x:Name="LoginEditor">
            <Editor.Behaviors>
                <behaviors:EventToCommandBehavior
                    EventName="Completed"
                    Command="{Binding EditorCompleted
                        Command}" />
            </Editor.Behaviors>
        </Editor>

        <Label
            FontSize="Small"
            IsVisible="{Binding EditorContentVisible}"
            LineBreakMode="WordWrap"
            Margin="10"
            Text="{Binding LostPasswordExcuse}"
            x:Name="EditorContents" />
    </VerticalStackLayout>
</ContentPage>
```

The Community Toolkit provides us with a much easier way to handle commands in `ViewModel`.

Popups and dialogs

It is not uncommon to want to alert the user to a condition or change or to get back a bit of data from the user with an alert, as shown in *Figure 4.22*:

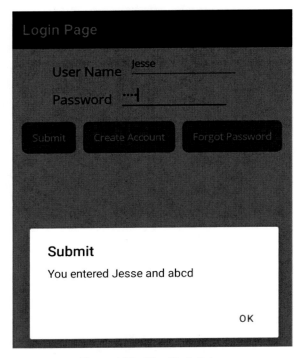

Figure 4.22 – The Alert dialog

To keep things clean, remove the Editor and its associated Label from `LoginPage.xaml` and remove the constructor and `ICommand` from `ViewModel`. We won't need them in the final version.

The `DisplayAlert` object can only be called from a page. Later, you'll see how to handle `SubmitCommand` on the Button in `ViewModel` and send a message to the page to show the alert. For now, let's keep things simple, and change the Button's `SubmitCommand` to an event:

```
<Button
    BackgroundColor="Gray"
    Clicked="OnSubmit"
    Margin="5"
    Text="Submit" />
```

The event handler is placed in the code-behind file. Notice the signature of the event handler:

```
private async void OnSubmit(object sender, EventArgs e)
 {

    await DisplayAlert(
```

```
    "Submit",
    $"You entered {vm.Name} and {vm.Password}",
    "OK");


}
```

The dialog in *Figure 4.22* displayed data but did not interact with the user (except to say to press **OK** to close the dialog). However, we can allow the user to make a choice and then record which button they press.

> **Event handler signature**
>
> OnSubmit wants to be async because you want to call DisplayAlert with await. With events (and only events) async is not an async Task but rather an async void. The parameters are always an Object type and EventArgs or a type derived from EventArgs. The first is typically named sender as this is the View that raised the event. EventArgs is empty and serves as the base class for specific types of arguments that some events pass into the event handler. Since we won't be using event handlers in the final code, you don't have to worry too much about this.

Here we've considered only one of the three types of alerts. Let's look at the other two next.

Presenting the user with a choice

While we're at it, let's look at the other two types of alerts. One asks the user to select one of two choices. We'll add that to the CreateAccount button just for now.

Let's add a clicked event to the OnCreate button:

```
<Button
    BackgroundColor="Gray"
    Clicked="OnCreate"
    Margin="5"
    Text="Create Account" />
```

And, to have a place to show the result, let's add a label after the closing HorizontalStackLayout tag:

```
<Label Text="Create account?" x:Name="CreateAccount" />
```

The code-behind file has the event handler, which will update our label:

```
private async void OnCreate(object sender, EventArgs e)
{
  CreateAccount.Text = (await DisplayAlert(
    "Create?",
    "Did you want to create an account?",
    "Yes",
    "No")).ToString();
}
```

DisplayAlert returns a Boolean, so we call ToString() to place it in the text field of the CreateAccount label. The dialog is shown in *Figure 4.23*:

Figure 4.23 – Using dialog to prompt a choice

We can go further and offer the user a series of choices. This is often referred to as a *wizard*, as it can be used to walk the user through a series of actions.

ActionSheet

The third variant of dialog is `ActionSheet`. Here we can put forward a number of choices and allow the user to select one. We'll attach this to an event handler for the **Forgot Password** button:

```
<Button
    BackgroundColor="Gray"
    Clicked="OnForgotPassword"
    Margin="5"
    Text="Forgot Password" />
```

Here's the event handler:

```
private async void OnForgotPassword(object sender,
    EventArgs e)
{
    CreateAccount.Text = (await DisplayActionSheet(   [1]
        "How can we solve this?",   [1]
        "Cancel",       [2]
        null,           [3]
        "Get new password",
        "Show me my hint",
        "Delete account"));
}
```

[1] The first parameter is the title.

[2] The second parameter is the text for the **Cancel** button.

[3] The third parameter is the text for the **OK** button. Since we don't need **OK**, we pass in `null`.

This is followed by a list of choices. *Figure 4.24* shows what this looks like when it runs:

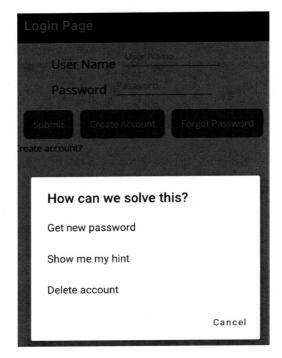

Figure 4.24 – ActionSheet

Finally, there are times when we want to allow the user to enter free-form data.

Displaying a prompt

The final variant of dialog provides a prompt to the user who can fill in a value. We'll need to modify the event handler for OnCreate to illustrate this:

```
private async void OnCreate(object sender, EventArgs e)
{
  CreateAccount.Text = await DisplayPromptAsync(
    title:"New Account",
    message:"How old are you?",
    placeholder:"Please enter your age",
    keyboard:Keyboard.Numeric,
    accept: "OK",
    cancel: "Cancel");

}
```

In this variant, it is common to use named parameters, as there are many options. *Figure 4.25* shows what this looks like:

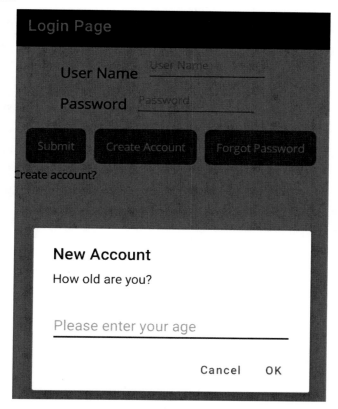

Figure 4.25 – Display prompt

Toast

A very popular alternative to dialog boxes is the *Toast* view. This is a popup that comes up from the bottom of the page (much like toast coming up out of a toaster), which displays its message and then disappears.

Let's modify the handler for OnCreate again, this time to display a toast:

```
private async void OnCreate(object sender, EventArgs e)
{
    CancellationTokenSource = [1]
      new CancellationTokenSource();
    var message = "Your account was created";
```

```
ToastDuration duration = ToastDuration.Short;   [2]
var fontSize = 14;
var toast = Toast.Make(message, duration, fontSize);
await toast.Show(cancellationTokenSource.Token);   [3]


}
```

When creating a Toast, you'll need cancellationToken. Fortunately, you can instantiate one from the static Token object from the CancellationTokenSource object [1] and [3].

You set the duration of how long the toast will be shown with the ToastDuration enumeration [2]. The choices are Long and Short.

Figure 4.26 shows the Toast:

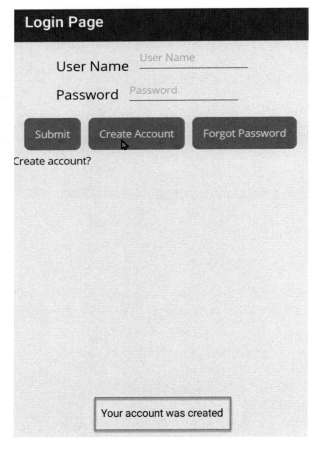

Figure 4.26 – Toast popup

Snackbar

If you need more control over the appearance of your Toast, you can use the closely related `Snackbar`. `Snackbar` not only has a plethora of options, it but it also has two steps. First is the display of the toast, and second is an (optional) action – that is, what do you want to do when the toast is dismissed? In this example, we'll display a dialog.

The cornucopia of options means that the event handler is a bit more extensive than usual:

```
private async void OnCreate(object sender, EventArgs e)
{
  CancellationTokenSource =   [1]
    new CancellationTokenSource();
  var message = "Your account was created";   [2]
  var dismissalText = "Click Here to Close the SnackBar";
    [3]
  TimeSpan duration = TimeSpan.FromSeconds(10);   [4]

  Action = async () =>   [5]
    await DisplayAlert(
      "Snackbar Dismissed!",
      "The user has dismissed the snackbar",
      "OK");

  var snackbarOptions = new SnackbarOptions   [6]
  {
    BackgroundColor = Colors.Red,
    TextColor = Colors.Yellow,
    ActionButtonTextColor = Colors.Black,   [7]
    CornerRadius = new CornerRadius(20),
    Font = Microsoft.Maui.Font.SystemFontOfSize(14),
    ActionButtonFont = Microsoft.Maui.Font
      .SystemFontOfSize(14)
  };

  var snackbar = Snackbar.Make(
    message,
    action,
```

```
        dismissalText,
        duration,
        snackbarOptions);


    await snackbar.Show(cancellationTokenSource.Token);


}
```

[1] We start by creating `CancellationTokenSource` as we did previously.

[2] Create a message to be displayed in the toast.

[3] Add a message that can be clicked on to dismiss the toast.

[4] Define how long you want the toast to be displayed. You can use any unit of time that `TimeSpan` supports (you could have the toast display for days!).

[5] The action is what will happen when the toast is dismissed.

[6] Here is where we set the characteristics of the toast.

[7] You can set the text color for the toast and for the dismissal text independently of each other.

Figure 4.27 shows what `Snackbar` looks like before we click on it:

Figure 4.27 – Snackbar

After the user clicks on the **Click Here to Close the SnackBar** text, SnackBar disappears, and the action is fired; in this case, the dialog box appears, as shown in *Figure 4.28*:

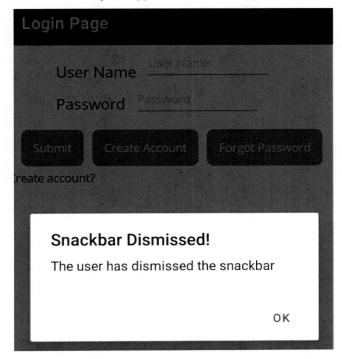

Figure 4.28 – The action after the snackbar is dismissed

.NET MAUI does not have a horizontal line control, but we can put the BoxView control to work as an excellent substitute.

BoxView

One of the simplest controls is BoxView, which simply draws a box on the page:

```
<BoxView
    Color="Red"
    CornerRadius="20"
    HeightRequest="125"
    WidthRequest="100" />
```

Figure 4.29 shows the `BoxView` control:

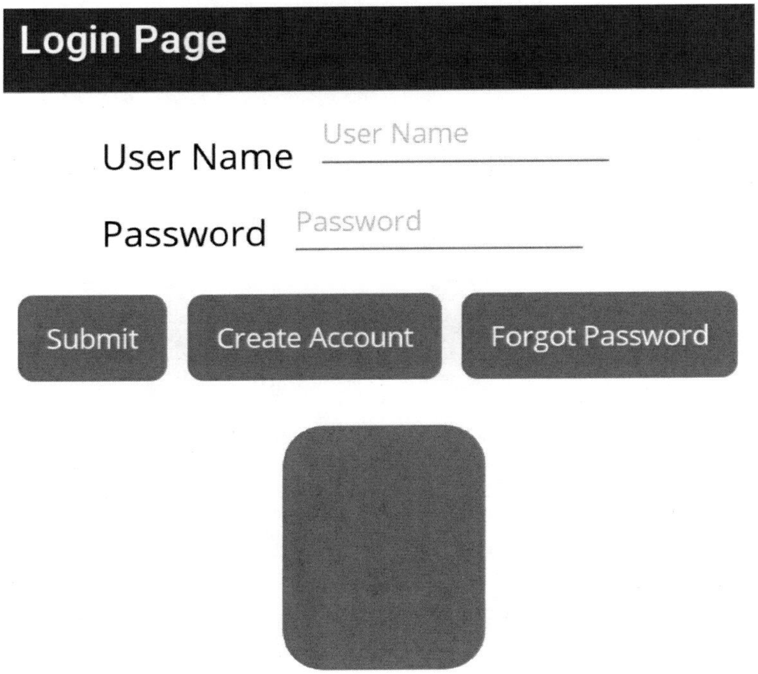

Figure 4.29 – A simple BoxView control

What good is this you ask? If you make the box height very small and the width very large, you get a nice line to divide your page. If we put the following after the **Password** entry, but before the buttons, we can neatly divide the page:

```
<BoxView
    Color="Red"
    HeightRequest="2"
    Margin="0,20"
    WidthRequest="400" />
```

Figure 4.30 shows what this looks like:

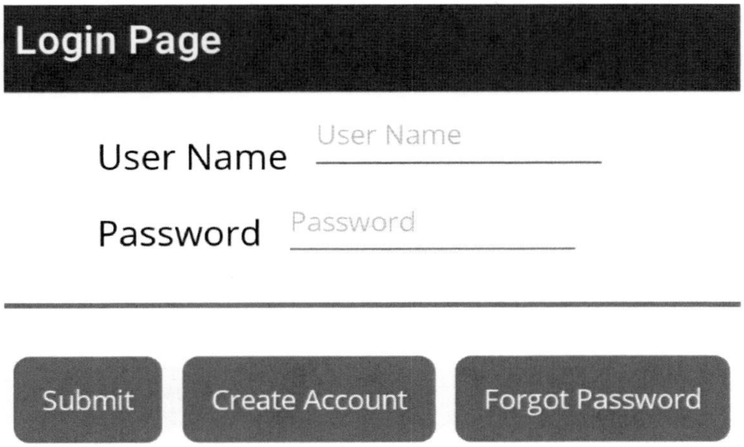

Login Page

User Name   *User Name*

Password   *Password*

Submit   Create Account   Forgot Password

Figure 4.30 – Using the BoxView control to draw a line

Many UI experts like to frame controls with a border, potentially with a *drop shadow*. To do this you'll want to use a Frame control.

Frame

If you wish to create a border around another control, you'll want to use a Frame control. Frame lets you define the color of the border, CornerRadius, and whether or not the frame has a shadow. Let's create a frame around the Password entry field:

```
<Frame
    BorderColor="Blue"
    CornerRadius="5">
    <Entry
        HorizontalOptions="End"
        IsPassword="True"
        Placeholder="Password"
        Text="{Binding Password}"
        WidthRequest="150" />
</Frame>
```

Figure 4.31 shows the result:

Figure 4.31 – Putting a frame around the Password entry

You control the color of the BoxView control and a number of other controls by painting the color using Brushes.

Brushes

You can fill in the color of any number of controls using a brush. The easiest place to see this in action is with a BoxView control, or with Frame.

There are three types of brushes, **Solid**, **Linear Gradient**, and **Radial Gradient**. Let's explore them in a bit more detail.

The Solid brush

The Solid Brush is used when you want to fill a control with a single color. Typically, the solid brush is implicit in the BackgroundColor property of the control, as we saw above when drawing the BoxView control.

LinearGradientBrush

LinearGradientBrush paints an area with a blend of two or more colors along a line called the gradient axis. You specify a start point and an endpoint, and then you specify stop points (where the colors switch) along the way.

The start and endpoints are relative to the borders of the painted area, with 0,0 being the upper left corner (and the default start) and 1,1 being the lower right (and the default stop).

To illustrate this, I'll move the frame from around the password to a space of its own:

```
<Frame
    BorderColor="Blue"
    CornerRadius="10"
    HasShadow="True"
    HeightRequest="100"
    WidthRequest="100">
    <Frame.Background>   [1]
        <LinearGradientBrush EndPoint="1,0"> [2]
            <GradientStop Color="Yellow" Offset="0.2" />
            [3]
            <GradientStop Color="Red" Offset="0.1" /> [4]
        </LinearGradientBrush>
    </Frame.Background>
</Frame>
```

[1] Here we create a Background property on Frame.

[2] Within that, create LinearGradientBrush.

Note that we specify EndPoint but not StartPoint, as we're using the default StartPoint of 0,0. By going from 0,0 to 1,0, we create a horizontal gradient.

[3] We have set the first GradientStop at 0.2.

[4] We set the second GradientStop at 0.1, giving us about twice as much yellow as red.

Figure 4.32 shows the result:

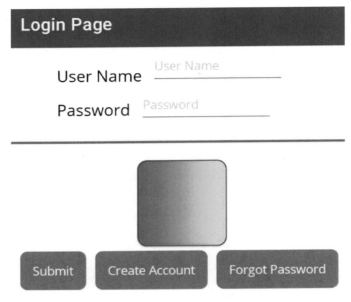

Figure 4.32 – LinearGradientBrush

> **Gradient stops**
>
> Gradient stops indicate the position along the gradient vector, ranging from 0 to 1. In short, the first gradient shown here is two-tenths of the way, and the second is one-tenth of the way along the gradient vector.

Gradients come in two flavors: linear, as shown in the previous example, and radial, as explained next.

RadialGradientBrush

If we do the same thing with `RadialGradientBrush`, our coordinates start at the center, which defaults to 0.5, 0.5, and we supply the radius as a double. The default value is 0.5. Let's reproduce `LinearGradient` shown previously using `RadialGradientBrush`:

```
<Frame
    BorderColor="Blue"
    CornerRadius="10"
    HasShadow="True"
    HeightRequest="100"
    WidthRequest="100">
```

```
    <Frame.Background>
        <RadialGradientBrush>
            <GradientStop Color="Yellow" Offset="0.2" />
            <GradientStop Color="Red" Offset="0.1" />
        </RadialGradientBrush>
    </Frame.Background>
</Frame>
```

Notice that we did not specify the center or the radius, so we are using the default values. *Figure 4.33* illustrates the result:

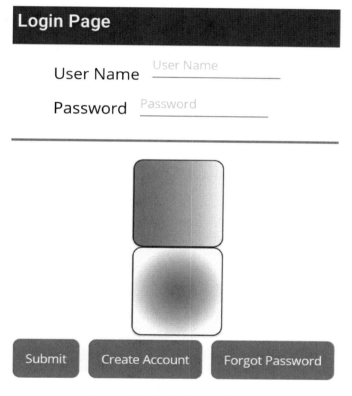

Figure 4.33 – RadialGradientBrush

With this, we've come to the end of a very important chapter.

Summary

This has been a long chapter, and we've covered many things, but if you break it down, the real topics were as follows:

- MVVM
- `DataBinding`
- Controls

Of course, controls are a pretty big topic, and we're not done. In the next chapter, we'll talk about layouts, but we'll also discuss how you style controls, animate controls, and more.

The 90% you use 90% of the time

I did not try to cover every control, nor did I cover all the properties of the controls we did see. That would have turned this book into an encyclopedia, and my goal is to show you the 90% of .NET MAUI that you use day in and day out. If you find you need a different property or a different control, well, that's what the (excellent) documentation is for. Just go to `https://bit.ly/Liberty-Maui`, or ask Google or your local AI agent, and you'll be able to find every nook and cranny.

The main takeaways from this chapter are:

- MVVM is the essential architecture for .NET MAUI. In MVVM, `Model` is the data (we've not seen this at work yet), `View` is the UI, and `ViewModel` is where all the logic is (or should be). We broke MVVM for much of this chapter and put the logic in the code-behind file, but that was only as a convenience and because we haven't, yet, talked about getting data into and out of pages.

- `DataBinding` is how you connect `ViewModel` to `View`. Rather than copying data from a property in `ViewModel` to a field in `View`, you bind that control to the property, and when the property's value changes, the control is automagically updated.

- There is a boatload of controls available to you and each is displayed as a native control on all of the supported platforms: iOS, Android, Windows, and macOS. The fact that they are emitted as native controls is tremendously important. Not only will they look right, but they will also be wicked fast.

- Anything you can declare in XAML you can declare in C#.

- You can take control over the appearance of each control so that they look the same on every platform – anything from having the same color all the way to looking identical. That is entirely up to you. It only depends on how many properties you set on each control.

Quiz

1. What are the advantages of MVVM?

2. How do you create the connection between the `View` class and `ViewModel` so that data binding will work?

3. What are two controls for entering data into a form?

4. What is the most common control for displaying data?

5. What is a `SnackBar`?

You try it

- Build a page that acts like a form

- Give it some prompts, entry fields, and buttons to accept the entry

- When the user fills in the field and clicks on the button, display a confirmation toast and show their entry in a label

- Add in an image, and for extra credit, enable that image to be clicked on and, when clicked on, display a congratulatory dialog box and/or toast (or if you are ambitious, use `SnackBar`!)

- Feel free to mix in additional controls

5

Advanced Controls

In the previous chapter, we looked at a number of controls and how to handle their events and commands. In this chapter, we'll look at moving the logic into `ViewModel` using commands and messaging. We'll then go on to cover Styles, which let you provide a uniform appearance to your controls with little effort.

One key feature of a well-designed user experience is that when something is going to take more than a second or so, you let the user know that the app is working on it so that it doesn't look like your app froze.

In this chapter, we will cover the following topics:

- Keeping the user informed of activity
- Moving event handling to `ViewModel`
- Sending and receiving messages
- Displaying collections
- Styles

Technical requirements

For this chapter, you will need Visual Studio. You can find the source code for this chapter here: `https://github.com/PacktPublishing/.NET-MAUI-for-C-Sharp-Developers/tree/MVVMAndControls`. If you want to follow along, continue with the project you were working on in *Chapter 4*.

Keeping the user informed of activity

There are two ways to let the user know that your application is working on something time-consuming:

- `ActivityIndicator`
- `ProgressBar`

`ActivityIndicator` essentially says, "I'm working on it, but I don't know how long it will take," whereas `ProgressBar` says, "I'm working on it, and I'm about halfway done." Let's explore each of these in a bit more detail.

ActivityIndicator

We'll start by adding `ActivityIndicator` to the login page below the Buttons:

```
<ActivityIndicator
    Color="Blue"
    IsRunning="{Binding ActivityIndicatorIsRunning}" />
```

Notice that the `IsRunning` property is bound to the `ActivityIndicatorIsRunning` property. That property is in `LoginViewModel` (you'll remember that we set that file as the binding context):

```
[ObservableProperty] private bool activityIndicatorIsRunning
  = true;
```

I've set its default value to `true`, so the activity indicator will be running when the page comes up. Let's shut it off after creating the account:

```
private async void OnCreate(object sender, EventArgs e)
{
  CancellationTokenSource =
    new CancellationTokenSource();
  var message = "Your account was created";
  var dismissalText = "Click Here to Close the SnackBar";
  TimeSpan duration = TimeSpan.FromSeconds(10);

  Action  = async () =>
    await DisplayAlert(
      "Snackbar Dismissed!",
```

```
      "The user has dismissed the snackbar",
      "OK");

  var snackbarOptions = new SnackbarOptions
  {
    BackgroundColor = Colors.Red,
    TextColor = Colors.Yellow,
    ActionButtonTextColor = Colors.Black,
    CornerRadius = new CornerRadius(20),
    Font = Microsoft.Maui.Font.SystemFontOfSize(14),
    ActionButtonFont = Microsoft.Maui.Font
      .SystemFontOfSize(14)
  };

  var snackbar = Snackbar.Make(
    message,
    action,
    dismissalText,
    duration,
    snackbarOptions);

  await snackbar.Show(cancellationTokenSource.Token);

  vm.ActivityIndicatorIsRunning = false;
}
```

Nothing has changed in the create page code except the addition of the final line. Here we reach into ViewModel and set the ActivityIndicatorIsRunning property to false. That should stop ActivityIndicator whose IsRunning property is bound to showActivityIndicator.

The result looks like *Figure 5.1*:

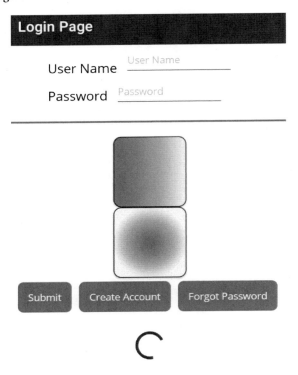

Figure 5.1 – ActivityIndicator

Working or hung?

Note that under some circumstances, your program might hang, yet the activity indicator will continue spinning. This can cause enormous confusion and frustration for your user. One way to escape that problem is to set a timer, and if the task doesn't complete in *n* seconds, you stop the indicator and, for example, display an error dialog. Of course, if everything is hung, you won't be able to do that, but typically, the indicator will have frozen as well.

`ActivityIndicator` is great, but it only tells the user that something is happening, not how far it has progressed in its task. That is what `ProgressBar` is for.

ProgressBar

`ProgressBar` divides a task into fractional parts (for example, percentages) and displays what part (fraction, percentage, and so on) has been completed. We've all seen progress bars: ideally, they move smoothly across the screen; in fact, they often move in fits and starts as the task they are tracking completes.

We're going to create a progress bar, but we are going to fake an action. That is, we'll progress the bar based on time rather than actual progress in a task. Nonetheless, the workings of `ProgressBar` will become evident.

To get started, let's comment out `ActivityIndicator` in `LoginPage.xaml`, and replace it with `ProgressBar`:

```
<!--<ActivityIndicator
    Color="Blue"
    IsRunning="{Binding ActivityIndicatorIsRunning}" />-->

<ProgressBar
    ProgressColor="Blue"
    x:Name="LoginProgressBar" />
```

Here we have declared `ProgressBar` with only two properties: its color and its name. The name allows us to refer to the bar in the code-behind. We would, of course, normally update `ProgressBar` based on data in the `ViewModel`, but for now, as we have done before, we'll do that work in the code-behind (`LoginPage.xaml.cs`).

Here is the code that will start and advance the progress bar based on the user clicking the **Submit** button:

```
private async void OnSubmit(object sender, EventArgs e)
{
  for (double i = 0.0; i < 1.0; i += 0.1)    [1]
  {
    await LoginProgressBar.ProgressTo(i, 500,
      Easing.Linear); [2]
  }
  await DisplayAlert(    [3]
    "Submit",
    $"You entered {vm.Name} and {vm.Password}",
    "OK");


}
```

[1] We will set the value of `ProgressBar` based on the value of the counter variable (`i`) in the `for` loop. The `ProgressBar` values range from 0 to 1, with the percentage or fraction of progress measured as values between those two numbers. Here, we initialize the counter variable to 0.0, and until it reaches the 1.0 value, we increment by one-tenth.

[2] Within the `for` loop, we call `ProgressTo` on `ProgressBar`. That method takes three values:

1. The value we want to progress to
2. The amount of time to get there, in milliseconds
3. The easing (see the following section)

[3] The action we'll take when the progress bar completes.

Another related feature is *Easing*, which refers to how quickly an action goes from start to full speed. Let's take a look at that in a bit more depth.

Easing

Easing refers to the pattern of how an item moves. For example, a train does not go from standing still in the station to racing along at 75 miles per hour all at once; it *eases* into the final speed. If you drew a graph of the acceleration, it would look like a sine wave, and two of the enumerated values of easing are, in fact, `SineIn` (for the pattern of starting up) and `SineOut` (for the pattern of coming back into the station).

In our case, however, we want the progress bar to move smoothly and at a constant speed, which is what `easing.Linear` does.

The net effect is that the progress bar will be animated across its entire course. We know that we are moving from 0 to 1 in tenths, and we know that we are taking half a second (500 milliseconds) to go each one-tenth of the way; thus, we know that the entire trip from 0.0 (nothing showing on the bar) to 1.0 (the bar fully filled with color) will take five seconds.

At the conclusion of our `for` loop, the dialog will pop up, giving a nice simulation of the completion of the task that the progress bar was tracking. A snapshot of that progress is shown in *Figure 5.2*:

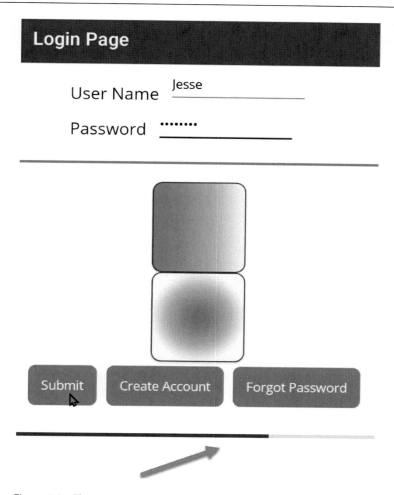

Figure 5.2 – The progress bar is about 75% of the way toward completion

For convenience and to keep things simple, we've been using the code-behind for event handling. Of course, as noted in *Chapter 3*, there are good reasons to use commands rather than events and to handle them in ViewModel. Let's look at that next.

Moving event handling to ViewModel

Suppose that when a Button is pressed, we want to handle that fact in the ViewModel, as is preferred by the **Model-View-ViewModel (MVVM)** pattern. However, one of the things we want to do, in response to that Button press, is to show a ProgressBar.

Handling things in `ViewModel` gets tricky when we want to interact with the **user interface** (**UI**). However, it can be done in a number of ways. Let's modify the **Submit** button, remove its `Clicked` event and add a command:

```
<Button
    BackgroundColor="Gray"
    Command="{Binding SubmitCommand}"
    Margin="5"
    Text="Submit" />
```

We'll create `RelayCommand` in `ViewModel` to handle the `Submit` Command:

```
[RelayCommand]
private async void Submit()
{

  for (var i = 0.0; i < 1.0; i += 0.1)
  {
    await LoginPage.LoginProgressBar.ProgressTo(i, 500,
      Easing.Linear); [1]
  }

  await Application.Current.MainPage.DisplayAlert(
    [2]
    "Submit",
    $"You entered {Name} and {Password}",
    "OK");

}
```

[1] Access `LoginProgressBar` on `LoginPage` (more later on how to do that) and call `ProgressTo` as we saw earlier.

[2] Access `MainPage` through the `Application` object and call `DisplayAlert`.

So, how are we going to access the `LoginProgressBar` in the UI? We need a static member of `LoginPage` to accomplish this. We'll pull the declaration of `LoginProgressBar` out of the **Extensible Application Markup Language** (**XAML**) and move it into the code-behind:

```
public static ProgressBar LoginProgressBar;
```

We need to be sure to initialize this in the constructor of `LoginPage`:

```
public LoginPage()
{
  LoginProgressBar = new ProgressBar();
```

We're going to need to refer to `StackLayout` if we want to add that to `ProgressBar`, so let's name it as follows:

```
<VerticalStackLayout x:Name="LoginStackLayout">
```

Now we're ready to add `ProgressBar` to the children of `StackLayout`. Here's the complete constructor:

```
public LoginPage()
{
  LoginProgressBar = new ProgressBar();
  InitializeComponent();  [1]
  LoginStackLayout.Children.Add(LoginProgressBar);  [2]
  BindingContext = vm;
}
```

[1] Notice that `InitializeComponent` comes before adding `ProgressBar` to the children of `StackLayout`. Until this is called, `LoginStackLayout` will be null.

[2] By calling `Add` here, `LoginProgressBar` is added to `LoginStackLayout` below the controls created in the XAML.

Huh? Let's take it step by step.

Breaking it down

Here is the order of what happens when you run this, enter your username and password, and click **Submit**:

1. `ProgressBar` is added to the page in the page constructor.

2. When you click on **Submit**, `SubmitCommand` is sent to `ViewModel`.

3. `ViewModel` handles that in `Submit`, `RelayCommand`.

4. In `RelayCommand`, it updates the (static) `LoginProgressBar`.

5. It then calls `DialogBox` through `MainPage`, which it has access to through the `Application` object.

This works beautifully but is a bit labored. The use of `Application.Current.MainPage` is not unusual, but the hoops we jumped through to access `ProgressBar` are. The solution to that is to use `Messaging`, which is covered next.

> **Visibility**
>
> It is generally considered best practice for `ViewModel` not to see aspects of the view (as it does here). In the next example, we will isolate the VM from the view.

Sending and receiving messages

Rather than reaching into `View`, we can have `ViewModel` signal `View` when it is time to display the dialog or other `View`-dependent element.

For example, suppose we want to show `Snackbar` when the user clicks on the **Create** button. Rather than using an event handler, we can use `Command` (which is preferred because it puts the logic into `ViewModel`). `ViewModel` might then massage data or otherwise do whatever it needs to do, and then signal `View` to display `Snackbar` by sending out a message to that effect.

The idea is that `ViewModel` publishes a message such as "anyone who has subscribed to this message, show a `Snackbar`" and the page subscribes to that message and so shows `Snackbar` when the message is received.

In some circumstances, there may be more than one **Subscriber**. For that matter, in some circumstances, more than one **Publisher** can send the same message, as shown in *Figure 5.3*:

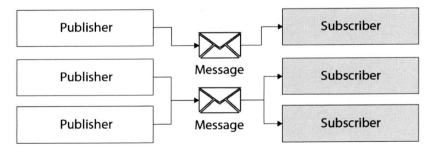

Figure 5.3 – Publish and Subscribe

> **Messaging center**
>
> .NET MAUI has a built-in messaging system, but it has been deprecated in favor of `WeakReferenceMessenger` provided in the .NET Community Toolkit MVVM, which we will cover next.

Getting started with WeakReferenceMessenger

To set this up, first create a class that will serve as the message. You can create this class anywhere that both `View` and `ViewModel` can see it. For convenience, I'll put it above the `LoginPage` class:

```
public partial class ConstructMessage {}
```

Next, in the `LoginPage` constructor, we need to register to receive such a message. Once you receive the message you might call a method, or alternatively, you'll use a Lambda expression to do the work.

To register to receive the message, use the `WeakReferenceMessenger's Register` method. Here is the code to do so:

```
WeakReferenceMessenger.Default.Register
  <ConstructMessage> (this, async ( m,e) =>
{
        // ...
});
```

What goes between the opening and closing braces is whatever you want to do when you receive that message. I've moved the code we were using in the event handler to here:

```
WeakReferenceMessenger.Default.Register
  <ConstructMessage> (this, async ( m,e) =>
{

  CancellationTokenSource =
    new CancellationTokenSource();
  var message = "Your account was created";
  var dismissalText = "Click Here to Close the
    SnackBar";
  TimeSpan duration = TimeSpan.FromSeconds(10);

  Action = async () =>
    await DisplayAlert(
      "Snackbar Dismissed!",
      message,
      "OK");

  var snackbarOptions = new SnackbarOptions
  {
```

```
            BackgroundColor = Colors.Red,
            TextColor = Colors.Yellow,
            ActionButtonTextColor = Colors.Black,
            CornerRadius = new CornerRadius(20),
            Font = Microsoft.Maui.Font.SystemFontOfSize(14),
            ActionButtonFont = Microsoft.Maui.Font
                .SystemFontOfSize(14)
        };

        var snackbar = Snackbar.Make(
            message,
            action,
            dismissalText,
            duration,
            snackbarOptions);

        await snackbar.Show(cancellationTokenSource.Token);

        vm.ActivityIndicatorIsRunning = false;

    });
```

Now, all we need to do is revise LoginPage.xaml so that the **Create Account** button calls a command in ViewModel, rather than an event handler in the code-behind:

```
<Button
    BackgroundColor="Gray"
    Command="{Binding CreateCommand}"
    Margin="5"
    Text="Create Account" />
```

This will invoke the Create relay method in the **ViewModel**

```
[RelayCommand]
private void Create()
{
  WeakReferenceMessenger.Default.Send(new CreateMessage());

}
```

`ViewModel` calls the `Send` method, sending in an instance of `ConstructMessage` as a signal to any registered listeners to take some action. The `Create` method might, before sending that message, do other work that is best done in `ViewModel` rather than code-behind.

This is a much cleaner way of *decoupling* `ViewModel` and `View` when we need to have logic in `ViewModel` take an action that can only be taken by `View`.

`WeakReferenceMessenger` can also be used to communicate from one `ViewModel` to another.

Finally, it is called `WeakReferenceMessenger` in distinction from stet `StrongReference-Messenger`. The advantage of `WeakReferenceMessenger`, and the reason it is generally what is chosen, is that it manages its own memory and cleanup, so you don't have to.

Creating the page in C#

Before moving on, and to reinforce the fact that anything you can do in XAML you can do in C#, here is the version of `LoginPage` that we will be using in Forget Me Not (ForgetMeNotDemo) written in C# (in the repo, this page is called `LoginCS`):

```
using CommunityToolkit.Maui.Markup;
using static CommunityToolkit.Maui.Markup.GridRowsColumns;
namespace ForgetMeNot.View
{

    class LoginCS : ContentPage
    {
        public LoginCS(LoginViewModel viewModel)    [1]
        {
            BindingContext = viewModel;

            var activity = new ActivityIndicator() [2]
            {
                HeightRequest = 50,
                Color = Color.FromRgb(0, 0, 0xF),
            };

            activity.IsEnabled = viewModel
                .ShowActivityIndicator; [3]
```

```
Content = new VerticalStackLayout()
{
    Children = [4]
    {
        activity,

        new Grid()   [5]
        {
            RowDefinitions = GridRowsColumns
                .Rows.Define(
                    (Row.Username,Auto),
                    (Row.Password,Auto),
                    (Row.Buttons, Auto)
                ),

            ColumnDefinitions = GridRowsColumns
                .Columns.Define(
                    (Column.Submit,Star),
                    (Column.Create, Star),
                    (Column.Forgot, Star)
                ),
            Children =
            {
                new Label()
                    .Text("User name")
                    .Row(Row.Username)
                        .Column(0), [6]

                new Entry()
                    .Placeholder("User name")
                    .Bind(Entry.TextProperty,
                        nameof(LoginViewModel
                            .LoginName))
                    .Row(Row.Username)
                        .Column(1)
                    .ColumnSpan(2),
```

```csharp
new Label()
    .Text("Password")
    .Row(Row.Password)
      .Column(0),

new Entry {IsPassword = true}
    .Placeholder("Password")
    .Bind(Entry.TextProperty,
    nameof(LoginViewModel
    .Password))
    .Row(Row.Password)
      .Column(1)
    .ColumnSpan(2),

new Button()
    .Text("Submit")
    .Row(Row.Buttons)
      .Column(Column.Submit)
    .BindCommand(nameof
      (LoginViewModel
        .DoLoginCommand)),
new Button()
    .Text("Create Account")
    .Row(Row.Buttons)
      .Column(Column.Create)
    .BindCommand(nameof
      (LoginViewModel
      .DoCreateAccountCommand)),
new Button()
    .Text("Forgot Password")
    .Row(Row.Buttons)
      .Column(Column.Forgot)
    .BindCommand(nameof
    (LoginViewModel
    .ForgotPasswordCommand))
```

```
                        }
                    }
                }
            };
        }
    }


    enum Row
    {
        Username,
        Password,
        Buttons
    }

    enum Column
    {
        Submit,
        Create,
        Forgot
    }

}
```

[1] We start by declaring the class and giving it `LoginViewModel`. This is done by *dependency injection*, a topic covered in detail in *Chapter 9*.

[2] `ActivityIndicator` is instantiated; it will be added to the page later.

[3] The `IsEnabled` property of `ActivityIndicator` is bound to a property in `ViewModel`.

[4] We add to `StackLayout` by adding to its `Children` collection.

[5] We haven't covered `Grid` yet, but you can see that it is a layout that has rows and columns. We'll look at it in greater depth in the next chapter.

[6] In `Grid`, each individual row and column can be given a name from `enumeration` or can be referred to by its zero-based index.

The key takeaway from this section is that you can certainly create all the controls and their commands and properties in C# as well as in XAML. I will continue to dip into C#, but I'm afraid it will drive you crazy to show each type in both, so again, for layout and controls, we'll focus predominantly on XAML – the standard approach for .NET MAUI.

Displaying collections

It is common to have a collection of data and to want to display it in a list, allowing the user to select one or more items and then do some work with those items. There are a couple of ways to do this in .NET MAUI, but the most common (and best) is to use `CollectionView`.

To see this at work, examine `Preferences.xaml` along with its code-behind `Preferences.xaml.cs` and ViewModel, `PreferencesViewModel.cs`. We will use this page extensively as we build Forget Me Not, but let's start slowly.

Our goal is to create a list of the user's preferences (shirt size, music genre, and so on). For that, we'll use `CollectionView`, and we'll, of course, need a collection to view. The page, when completed, will look much like this:

Figure 5.4 – The Preferences page

Rather than each line being a unique object, we'll create one type that we can show repeatedly. In the Model folder, create a Preference class:

```
namespace ForgetMeNotDemo.Model;


[ObservableObject]
public partial class Preference
{
    [ObservableProperty] private string preferencePrompt;
    [ObservableProperty] private string preferenceValue;


}
```

> **Partial classes**
> In .NET MAUI virtually all classes are *partial* to support the Community Toolkit code.

Preference has only two properties, both strings. The PreferencePrompt string will hold the text on the left of the page, and the PreferenceValue string will hold the user's preference on the right side.

The first thing we need is a collection of these Preference objects. To get that, we're going to build a Service, whose job, eventually, will be to interact with the API and get us our list of Preference objects. Perform the following steps:

1. Create a new folder named Services.

2. In Services, create a PreferenceService class.

3. Inside that file add a GetPreferences method.

Here's the code:

```
public class PreferenceService
{
  public async Task<List<Preference>> GetPreferences()
  {
    return await GetPreferencesMock();
  }

  private async Task<List<Preference>> GetPreferencesMock(
  {
```

```
    return null;
  }
}
```

ViewModel will call GetPreferences on the service and get back a list of the Preference objects. We'll turn to how PreferenceService gets those objects in just a bit.

Back in PreferencesViewModel, do the following:

```
[ObservableObject]
public partial class PreferencesViewModel
{
    [ObservableProperty] private List<Preference>
      preferences;
    private readonly PreferenceService service;  [1]

    public PreferencesViewModel()
    {
      service = new();  [2]
    }

    public async Task Init()
    {
      Preferences = await service.GetPreferences();  [3]
    }

}
```

[1] Declare an instance of PreferenceService

[2] Initialize it in the constructor

[3] In the Init method, fill the Preferences collection with what you get back from the service

Dependency injection

In *Chapter 9*, we will review dependency injection. At that point, we'll pass in a PreferenceService interface and let the InversionOfControl container supply the service for us. If that didn't make sense to you, no problem; it will all become clear in *Chapter 9*.

So, who instantiates `ViewModel` and calls `Init`? For that, we turn to the code-behind of the `PreferencesPage` class:

```
public partial class PreferencesPage : ContentPage
{
  private PreferencesViewModel vm;
  public Preferences()
  {
    vm = new PreferencesViewModel();
    BindingContext = vm;
    InitializeComponent();
  }

  protected override async void OnAppearing()
  {
    base.OnAppearing();
    await vm.Init();
  }
}
```

Naming the ViewModel vm

I'm not big on using acronyms in code, and would normally have named the local instance of `ViewModel`. But using *vm* is such a convention in .NET MAUI (going back to `Xamarin.Forms`) that I indulge myself.

In .NET MAUI, the two life cycle events you will often want control over are when the page is first being shown (`OnAppearing`) and when it is being shut down (`OnDisappearing`). Let's explore this next.

Overriding OnAppearing

Every time a page appears, its `OnAppearing` method is called. We override that method so that we can call vm.`Init()`. We do this because `Init` is asynchronous, and while we can make `OnAppearing` asynchronous using the `async` keyword, we can't do that with the constructor.

`OnInit()`, in turn, calls `GetPreferences` on the service and gets back a collection of the `Preference` objects.

Understanding how the service works

In time, our PreferenceService's GetPreferences method will call into our API to get the list of preferences from our database, which will be stored in the cloud. For now, it will call GetPreferencesMock, which will handcraft the list and return it to us.

Here's an excerpt from the file:

```
public class PreferenceService
{
  public async Task<List<Preference>> GetPreferences()
  {
    return await GetPreferencesMock();
  }

  private async Task<List<Preference>> GetPreferencesMock()
  {
    List<Preference> preferences = new()
    {
      new Preference()
      {
        PreferencePrompt = "Shirt Size",
        PreferenceValue = ""
      },
      new Preference()
      {
        PreferencePrompt = "Favorite Music Genre",
        PreferenceValue = ""
      },
      new Preference()
      {
        PreferencePrompt = "Favorite Color",
        PreferenceValue = ""
      },
      new Preference()
      {
        PreferencePrompt = "Favorite Food",
        PreferenceValue = ""
```

```
      },
      new Preference()
      {
        PreferencePrompt = "Favorite Movie",
        PreferenceValue = ""
      },
//…
    };
    return preferences;
  }
}
```

The result is a collection of `Preference` objects. Let's look at how to display that collection.

Displaying the collection of Preference objects

Now that we have a collection of `Preference` objects in `ViewModel`, we can create our page:

```xml
<?xml version="1.0" encoding="utf-8" ?>
<ContentPage xmlns="http://schemas.microsoft.com/
  dotnet/2021/maui"
            xmlns:x="http://schemas.microsoft.com/
              winfx/2009/xaml"
            x:Class="ForgetMeNotDemo.View.PreferencesPage"
            Title="Preferences">
    <ScrollView>
        <VerticalStackLayout>
            <Label
                Margin="5"
                Padding="5"
                HorizontalOptions="Center"
                LineBreakMode="WordWrap"    [1]
                Text="Please fill in as many preferences as
                you care to. &#10; &#10;The fields are
                'free form,' fill in anything you like.
                Remember, the more information you provide
                to your buddies the better they will be
                able to match to what you like. Each of the
```

```
            categories can be edited for your
            needs.&#10; &#10; Save as frequently as you
            like, and to edit, just change the value
            you entered and press save." />
<Button
    Margin="30,20,0,0"
    Clicked="SavePreferences"       [2]
    Command="{Binding SavePreferencesCommand}"
      [3]
    Text="Save" />
<CollectionView
    Margin="20,20,10,10"
    ItemsSource="{Binding Preferences}" [4]
    SelectionMode="None">           [5]
    <CollectionView.ItemTemplate>   [6]
        <DataTemplate>
            <Grid ColumnDefinitions="*,2*">
                <Entry  [7]
                    Grid.Column="0"
                    FontSize="10"
                    HorizontalOptions="Start"
                    HorizontalTextAlignment=
                      "Start"
                    Text="{Binding
                    PreferencePrompt,
                      Mode=TwoWay}" [8]
                    TextColor="{OnPlatform
                      Black,   [9]
                      iOS=White}" />
                <Entry
                    Grid.Column="1"
                    FontSize="10"
                    HeightRequest="32"
                    HorizontalOptions="Start"
                    HorizontalTextAlignment=
                      "Start"
```

```
                                         Text="{Binding
                                          PreferenceValue,
                                            Mode=TwoWay}"
                                         TextColor="{OnPlatform
                                            Black,
                                              iOS=White}"
                                         WidthRequest="350" />
                        </Grid>
                    </DataTemplate>
                </CollectionView.ItemTemplate>
            </CollectionView>

            <Button
                Margin="30,20,0,0"
                Clicked="SavePreferences"
                Command="{Binding SavePreferencesCommand}"
                Text="Save" />

        </VerticalStackLayout>
    </ScrollView>
</ContentPage>
```

There is much to see in this listing. Let's take things one by one:

[1] Label has multiple lines; we've seen this before. We set LineBreakMode to WordWrap so that we break the lines between words. Notice the use of
, which forces a line break.

[2] The **Save** button is very unusual as it has a click event handler as well as a command! The click event handler will handle showing the toast.

[3] The command will be handled in ViewModel and will call the Save method in the service (which we will not implement just yet).

[4] The ItemsSource property points to the collection that CollectionView will display. In our case, that is the Preferences collection in ViewModel.

[5] SelectionMode is set to None, as we won't be selecting items in this display. We will be editing items and then pressing **Save** to save the changes.

[6] An item template says, "here is how I want you to display each item in the collection, one by one."

[7] Interestingly, we are using Entry for the prompt. This allows the user to change the prompt, which is what we want. We can't anticipate every category, so we create a number of them, but we let the user tweak the list as needed.

[8] Not only will we be displaying the value of the prompt from the database, but we'll want to write back whatever the user enters as well. Thus, we mark the text as two-way (that is, data > View and View > data)

[9] We've not seen onPlatform before. This says, "always use this value except, on this platform, use this other value." Here we are saying that the text color is Black, except on Ios, where it is White.

The code-behind

You'll remember that we are not only handling the command in ViewModel but we're also handling the Clicked event in the code-behind. Here is the rest of PreferencesPage.xaml.cs:

```
public void SavePreferences(object sender, EventArgs e)
{
    ShowToast();
}


private async Task ShowToast()
{
    var cancellationTokenSource = new
        CancellationTokenSource();
    var message = "Your preferences were saved";
    ToastDuration duration = ToastDuration.Short;
    var fontSize = 14;
    var toast = Toast.Make(message, duration,
        fontSize);
    await toast.Show(cancellationTokenSource.Token);


}
```

The event handler just calls the ShowToast method, which then does its thing, as described earlier.

This way, when the list of preferences is saved, the toast notifies the user that all went well.

> **Did it all go well?**
>
> In the code shown, we just assume that it all went well. To do this properly, we'd want `ViewModel` to wait for confirmation from the API that the operation was completed successfully, and then it would send a message to the code-behind, which would then, and only then, display the toast.

Before we go any further, open `AppShell.xaml` and change the startup as follows:

```
<ShellContent
    Title="Home"
    ContentTemplate="{DataTemplate
      view1:PreferencesPage}"
    Route="PreferencesPage" />
```

Once we get to *Chapter 7*, we can stop this silliness and just navigate to the page we want.

The effect of all of this is shown in *Figure 5.5*:

Figure 5.5 – The Preferences page

A few quick things to note in *Figure 5.5*. The fields on the left have been underlined, indicating that they are entry objects, not labels, and thus can be modified. The top arrow points to the fact that the fields are free-form, and the user can enter whatever they want, and the lower arrow points to the toast.

So far, we've been setting numerous properties on our UI controls. Often, we've had to repeat the same properties on various instances of the same type of control. There is a better way: styles, which we'll cover next.

Styles

Styles allow you to provide a uniform look to your controls by putting all the details in one place.

You create a style for a control type (for example, `Button`), and that style is applied to all controls of that type (refer to the *Explicit versus implicit styles* section). You can also base a style on an existing style, extending or modifying the original.

Styles can be stored on the page that uses the control, or they can be stored at the application level. In either case, they are created inside `ResourceDictionary`, typically declared at the top of the file. To make them available at the application level, just put them in `App.xaml`.

> **Where to put your styles**
>
> If you are only going to use the styles on objects on a single page, it makes sense to put the styles in the resources of that page. If you want to be able to reuse these styles on multiple pages, then you will want them in `App.xaml`.

As an example, let's return to the **Login** page and create `ResourceDictionary` and our first styles. Place this code at the very top of the file, just below the `ContentPage` element:

```
<ContentPage.Resources>
    <Style TargetType="Label">
        <Setter Property="FontSize" Value="Medium"/>
        <Setter Property="HorizontalOptions"
          Value="Start"/>
        <Setter Property="Margin" Value="10"/>
        <Setter Property="VerticalOptions"
          Value="Center"/>
        <Setter Property="VerticalTextAlignment"
          Value="Center"/>
    </Style>
</ContentPage.Resources>
```

You can see that we have created a style for the labels on the page. In that style, we have set a number of properties with their values. This will be applied to every `Label` because this is an implicit style, as described next.

The key to the use of styles is that they greatly simplify the controls they are applied to. For example, the labels now look like this:

```
<Label
    Text="User Name" />
```

They are no longer cluttered with all the style information that has been centralized in `ResourceDictionary`. This not only makes for cleaner XAML, but if you later decide to change one of these values, you do so in one place rather than throughout the page. Thus, the same clean code guideline that applies to C# (don't repeat yourself) applies to styles.

There are two types of styles: implicit and explicit. **Implicit styles** are applied to every control of `TargetType`, as we saw earlier. **Explicit styles** can be applied to controls individually. Let us explore this in more detail next.

Explicit versus implicit styles

To make a style explicit, you give it a key, as shown here:

```
<Style TargetType="Label" x:Key="LargeLabel">
    <Setter Property="FontSize" Value="Large" />
    <Setter Property="HorizontalOptions" Value="Start" />
    <Setter Property="Margin" Value="10" />
    <Setter Property="VerticalOptions" Value="Center" />
    <Setter Property="VerticalTextAlignment" Value="Center"
      />
</Style>
<Style TargetType="Label" x:Key="SmallLabel">
    <Setter Property="FontSize" Value="Small" />
    <Setter Property="HorizontalOptions" Value="Start" />
    <Setter Property="Margin" Value="10" />
    <Setter Property="VerticalOptions" Value="Center" />
    <Setter Property="VerticalTextAlignment" Value="Center"
      />
</Style>
```

You can now pick which of these styles you want to apply to `Label` based on that key:

```
<Label
    Text="User Name"
    Style="{StaticResource LargeLabel}"/>
<Label
    Text="Password"
    Style="{StaticResource SmallLabel}"/>
```

The result is shown in *Figure 5.6*:

Login Page

User Name   User Name

Password   Password

Figure 5.6 – Explicit styles applied

> **Overriding the style in the control**
>
> If you have a style that you want to use on all of your (for example) labels, but you have one `Label` that needs one or two properties to be different, one way to handle that is just to make the change in that `Label`. Properties assigned directly to the control override those of the style. On the other hand, if you have sets of controls that need nearly the same properties but differ in some ways, then you want to use style inheritance, which is covered next.

Style inheritance or BasedOn

The construct for `LargeLabel` and `SmallLabel` has a lot of duplication. You can refactor this to use a base style and then just add the changes in your explicit styles. Here's an example:

```
<Style TargetType="Label">  [1]
    <Setter Property="FontSize" Value="Medium" />
    <Setter Property="HorizontalOptions" Value="Start" />
    <Setter Property="Margin" Value="10" />
    <Setter Property="VerticalOptions" Value="Center" />
    <Setter Property="VerticalTextAlignment"
      Value="Center" />
```

```
</Style>
<Style TargetType="Label" x:Key="BaseExplicitLabel"> [2]
    <Setter Property="FontSize" Value="Medium" />
    <Setter Property="HorizontalOptions" Value="Start" />
    <Setter Property="Margin" Value="10" />
    <Setter Property="VerticalOptions" Value="Center" />
    <Setter Property="VerticalTextAlignment"
      Value="Center" />
</Style>

<Style
    TargetType="Label"
    x:Key="LargeLabel"
    BasedOn="{StaticResource BaseExplicitLabel}"> [3]
    <Setter Property="FontSize" Value="Large" />
</Style>
<Style
    TargetType="Label"
    x:Key="SmallLabel"
    BasedOn="{StaticResource BaseExplicitLabel}">
    <Setter Property="FontSize" Value="Small" />
</Style>
            <Label
                Style="{StaticResource LargeLabel}" [4]
                Text="User Name" />
```

[1] An implicit label style

[2] A style created to be the base style for other styles

[3] A derived style that uses properties from the base style

[4] Using the derived style

> **Derived styles**
>
> Note that derived styles can add new properties (as was done here), they can override values in the base style, or both. Notice also that we refactored the styles, but did not have to refactor Label that uses it.

Summary

In this chapter, we dove deeper into some of the more advanced aspects of .NET MAUI controls. We looked at the `Activity` element as well as `ProgressBar`. We went on to look at moving command handling into `ViewModel` and using messages to communicate between `ViewModel` and `View`.

We ended the chapter by looking at styles and how they can be used to provide a uniform appearance to the UI and how we can refactor duplication out of similar styles by using style inheritance (`BasedOn`).

In the next chapter, we'll look at how we lay out `controls` on the page, moving beyond the simple `StackLayouts` we've been using so far.

Quiz

1. What is the difference between `ActivityIndicator` and `ProgressBar`?
2. What is the difference between an event and a command?
3. What is `WeakReferenceManager`?
4. Why would you use a style?
5. How do you refactor common properties in styles?

You try it

Create a small form that pretends to gather information on the user to create a profile (name, age, address, and so on). Add an image you can tap on and two buttons: one to accept the entered info and one to cancel it.

If the user taps on the image, put up a dialog box with a message, but handle the tap itself in `ViewModel`.

Handle the button clicks in `ViewModel`. On clicking **Cancel**, put up a toast acknowledging the cancellation. On clicking **OK**, use `Snackbar` to show what info they have saved, nicely formatted.

6
Layout

In the previous two chapters, we looked at controls – the widgets that ask for and display data – but widgets need to be positioned on the page, with a process called the layout. Layout is the difference between an ugly app and a professional-looking one.

There are several layout controls available to you, which we will cover in this chapter:

- Vertical and horizontal stack layouts
- `Grid`
- Scrolling
- Flex layout

> **I am not a designer**
>
> For a page to look professional, a designer must work with the developer, specifying not only where to put the controls but also the font size, font, margins, and so on. I am not a designer, and the pages we'll create are for illustration purposes only; they will not be pretty.

Technical requirements

The source code for this chapter can be found in the GitHub repository under this branch: `https://github.com/PacktPublishing/.NET-MAUI-for-C-Sharp-Developers/tree/Layouts`

Stack layouts

Stack layouts allow you to stack one control on top of another or next to one another. They come in three flavors:

- `StackLayout`
- `VerticalStackLayout`
- `HorizontalStackLayout`

The first of these is for backward compatibility with `Xamarin.Forms` and is effectively deprecated; the other two are far more performant.

We've seen `VerticalStackLayout` and `HorizontalStackLayout` at work already. As the name indicates, `VerticalStackLayout` places one control *on top of* another, while `HorizontalStackLayout` places them side by side. Using `margins` (the space between objects) and `padding` (the space around an object), you can tweak a nice enough layout with just these controls:

```
<VerticalStackLayout x:Name="LoginStackLayout">
    <HorizontalStackLayout WidthRequest="300">
        <Label
            Style="{StaticResource LargeLabel}"
            Text="User Name" />
        <Entry
            HorizontalOptions="End"
            Placeholder="User Name"
            Text="{Binding Name}"
            WidthRequest="150" />
    </HorizontalStackLayout>
    <HorizontalStackLayout WidthRequest="300">
        <Label
            Style="{StaticResource SmallLabel}"
            Text="Password" />
        <Entry
            HorizontalOptions="End"
            IsPassword="True"
            Placeholder="Password"
            Text="{Binding Password}"
            WidthRequest="150" />
    </HorizontalStackLayout>
```

```
<BoxView
    Color="Red"
    HeightRequest="2"
    Margin="0,20"
    WidthRequest="400" />
```

Here, on the LoginPage page, we start with a VerticalStackLayout object, which will contain everything below it until the closing </VerticalStackLayout> tag. Immediately, we declare a HorizontalStackLayout object, which contains a Label (acting as a prompt) and an Entry (gathering the name from the user).

Below HorizontalStackLayout is a second HorizontalStackLayout and below that is a BoxView. In short, VerticalStackLayout continues to stack views on top of each other.

While this is fine for a very simple layout, it has its limitations. Working with VerticalStackLayout and HorizontalStackLayout on complicated layouts becomes difficult after a short while.

Enter the most powerful layout of them all: Grid.

Grid

Nothing comes close to Grid for flexibility, although its basic use is dead simple. A grid consists of rows and columns. You define the size of each and then fill in the resulting boxes.

By default, all the columns are the same width, and all the rows are the same height. Rows and columns are identified (by default) by their offset starting at column 0, row 0. You can leave out the 0 (it is the default value) but I advise against doing so for readability. (This is the same reason I mark private methods and classes with the private keyword.)

We can recreate the LoginPage page using Grid. Let's look at the first approximation in full (I've left out the resources section, as it is unchanged):

```
<?xml version="1.0" encoding="utf-8" ?>
<ContentPage
    Title="Login Page"
    x:Class="ForgetMeNotDemo.View.LoginPage"
    xmlns="http://schemas.microsoft.com/dotnet/2021/maui"
    xmlns:behaviors="http://schemas.microsoft.com/dotnet
     /2022/maui/toolkit"
    xmlns:x="http://schemas.microsoft.com/winfx/2009/xaml">
    <VerticalStackLayout x:Name="LoginStackLayout">     [1]
        <Grid   [2]
```

```
ColumnDefinitions="*,*,*"  [3]
RowDefinitions="*,*,*,*,*"  [4]
x:Name="LoginGrid">
<Label
    Grid.Column="0"  [5]
    Grid.Row="0"  [6]
    HorizontalOptions="End" [7]
    Margin="5,20,0,10"
    Text="User Name"
    VerticalOptions="Center" [8] />
<Entry
    Grid.Column="1"
    Grid.ColumnSpan="2" [9]
    Grid.Row="0"
    HorizontalOptions="Center"
    Margin="5,20,0,10"
    Placeholder="User Name"
    Text="{Binding Name}"
    VerticalOptions="End"
    WidthRequest="150" />
<Label                       [10]
    Grid.Column="0"
    Grid.Row="1"
    HorizontalOptions="End"
    Margin="5,10"
    Text="Password"
    VerticalOptions="Center" />
<Entry
    Grid.Column="1"
    Grid.ColumnSpan="2"
    Grid.Row="1"
    HorizontalOptions="Center"
    IsPassword="True"
    Placeholder="Password"
    Text="{Binding Password}"
    VerticalOptions="Start"
```

```
                WidthRequest="150" />
        <BoxView
            Color="Red"
            Grid.Column="0"
            Grid.ColumnSpan="3"  [11]
            Grid.Row="2"
            HeightRequest="2"
            Margin="0,10"
            WidthRequest="400" />
```

The next thing to add is the frames:

```
        <Frame
            BorderColor="Blue"
            CornerRadius="10"
            Grid.Column="0"
            Grid.Row="3"
            HasShadow="True"
            HeightRequest="50"
            WidthRequest="50">
            <Frame.Background>
                <LinearGradientBrush EndPoint="1,0">
                    <GradientStop Color="Yellow"
Offset="0.2" />

                    <GradientStop Color="Red"
                        Offset="0.1" />
                </LinearGradientBrush>
            </Frame.Background>
        </Frame>

        <Frame
            BorderColor="Blue"
            CornerRadius="10"
            Grid.Column="1"
            Grid.ColumnSpan="2"
```

```
        Grid.Row="3"
        HasShadow="True"
        HeightRequest="50"
        WidthRequest="100">
        <Frame.Background>
            <RadialGradientBrush>
                <GradientStop Color="Yellow"
                    Offset="0.2" />
                <GradientStop Color="Red"
                    Offset="0.1" />
            </RadialGradientBrush>
        </Frame.Background>
    </Frame>
```

With that in place, we can add the three buttons and then close Grid and VerticalStackLayout:

```
<Button
    BackgroundColor="Gray"
    Command="{Binding SubmitCommand}"
    Grid.Column="0"
    Grid.Row="4"
    Margin="5"
    Text="Submit" />
<Button
    BackgroundColor="Gray"
    Command="{Binding CreateCommand}"
    Grid.Column="1"
    Grid.Row="4"
    Margin="5"
    Text="Create Account" />
<Button
    BackgroundColor="Gray"
    Clicked="OnForgotPassword"
    Grid.Column="2"
    Grid.Row="4"
    Margin="5"
    Text="Forgot Password" />
```

```
            <Label
                Grid.Column="0"
                Grid.ColumnSpan="3"
                Grid.Row="5"
                Text="
                x:Name="CreateAccount" />
        </Grid>
    </VerticalStackLayout>
</ContentPage>
```

[1] We'll put `Grid` inside a `VerticalStackLayout` so that we can add the `ProgressBar` below the grid (adding it to `VerticalStackLayout`'s `Children` collection, which will have only two members: `Grid` and `ProgressBar`).

[2] We declare `Grid` with the keyword.

[3] We declare three columns of equal size (`*`, `*`, `*`).

"Some have stars upon thars" – Dr. Seuss

Stars don't make much difference when they are all the same size, but if, for example, we wanted the first to be twice as big as the others, we would write the following:

`ColumnDefinitions="2*,*,*"`

In that case, the column would be divided into four equal parts and the first column would get two of them and the other columns one each. The result is that the first column would be twice as wide as the others.

---

[4] Similarly, we declare five rows of equal size.

[5] We place the Label inside column 0.

[6] We place the Label inside row 0.

[7] The horizontal option is with respect to the column the control is in.

[8] The vertical option is with respect to the row the control is in.

[9] A control can span across more than one column. In this case, the entry begins at column 1 and runs for a column span of 2 (that is, it occupies both column 1 and 2).

[10] Notice that we don't need a `HorizontalStackLayout` because the position of the prompt with respect to the entry is determined by what columns they are in and their horizontal options (for example, start, center, or end).

[11] `BoxView` wants to stretch across the entire grid and so starts at column 0 and has a column span of 3.

Notice that nothing else needs to change. I manipulated the margins and vertical options to get the *pixel-perfect* alignment I was looking for, but other than that, the XAML remains the same.

One other thing to note is that we have an opportunity to factor out the vertical and horizontal options and the margins into the styles.

The result of converting the `StackLayout` into this grid is shown in *Figure 6.1*.

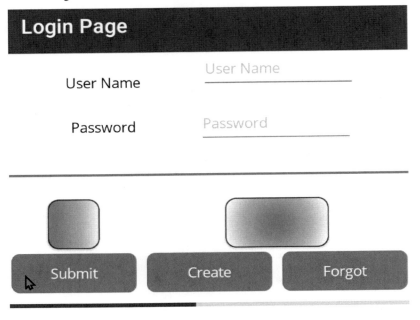

Figure 6.1 – First grid layout

Notice that the `ProgressBar` is still shown. It is added to `VerticalStackLayout` in the code-behind as it was previously.

Sizing rows and columns

`RowHeight` and `ColumnWidth` can be defined in one of three ways:

1. *absolute*: A value in DIUs
2. *auto*: Auto-sized based on the cell contents
3. *Stars*: As shown earlier, with proportional allocation

Currently, the top of the Grid looks like this:

```
<Grid   [2]
    ColumnDefinitions="*,*,*"
    RowDefinitions="*,*,*,*,*"
```

We could have used auto to say that each control will take up the amount of room it needs on each row:

```
<Grid   [2]
    ColumnDefinitions="*,*,*"
    RowDefinitions="auto,auto,auto,auto,auto"
```

Let's also set the height of the frames to 150. auto allocates enough room for the newly enlarged frames, as illustrated in *Figure 6.2*.

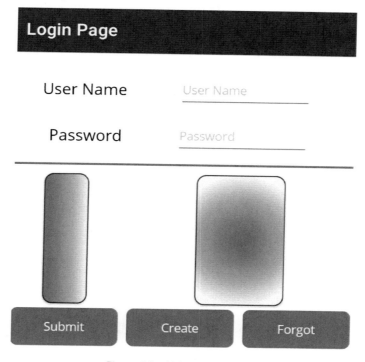

Figure 6.2 – Using auto-sizing

> **Best practice – minimize use of auto**
>
> Microsoft recommends minimizing the use of auto as it is less performant (the layout engine has to perform additional calculations). That being said, at times, it is very useful, especially when the size of the object will be determined at runtime.

We could rewrite the rows shown before as follows:

```
<Grid
    ColumnDefinitions="*,*,*"
    RowDefinitions="*,*,auto,auto,50,auto"
```

The calculation now would be to find the actual size of the three auto rows and add 50 Device-Independent Units, for the fifth row. Then, we take what is left in the grid size, and divide it equally between the first and second rows. The result is shown in the following figure:

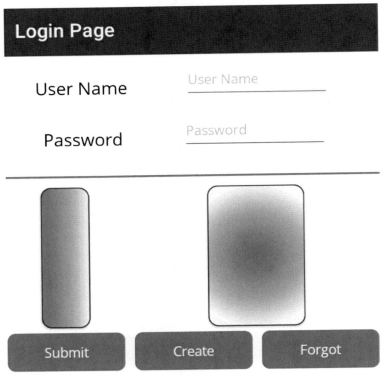

Figure 6.3 – Combining stars, absolute, and auto

As you can see, by mixing and matching, you can create an awful-looking UI. On the other hand, given to a designer, these three options (absolute, stars, and auto) can be used to create beautiful UIs with precise control over sizing.

Named rows and columns

In the preceding code, we referred to each row and column by its zero-based offset. Thus, the frames were in `Grid.row[3]` in `Grid.column[0]` and `Grid.column[1]`. With large grids, this can become confusing and difficult to manage.

In C#, .NET MAUI offers you the option of naming your rows and columns using an enumeration. To see this, let's create an alternative login page, entirely in C#, and then take a look at it.

We'll simplify the page slightly, taking out `BoxView` and `Frame`, to keep our focus on the manipulation of the rows and columns.

First, we are going to define enumerations, which will serve as the names of our rows and columns, respectively:

```
enum Row
{
   Username,
   Password,
   Buttons
}

enum Column
{
   Submit,
   Create,
   Forgot
}
```

What you use for these names is entirely up to you; typically, you'll use something that describes what goes into those rows and columns. Thus, here, my first row will hold `Username`, my second row will hold `Password`, and my third row will hold our three `Buttons`.

Notice that the columns are named after the type of buttons. That makes it difficult (or confusing) to use those columns with these rows. We'll solve that by falling back to using offsets on those rows.

Here is the complete class, which I named `LoginCS.cs`:

```
class LoginCS : ContentPage
{
   public LoginCS()    [1]
   {
```

```
BindingContext = new LoginViewModel();

Content = new VerticalStackLayout() [2]
{
  Children =
              {
                new Grid()   [3]
                {
                        RowDefinitions = GridRowsColumns
                            .Rows.Define(
                            (Row.Username,Auto), [4]
                            (Row.Password,Auto),
                            (Row.Buttons, Auto)
                            ),

                        ColumnDefinitions = GridRowsColumns
                            .Columns.Define(
                            (Column.Submit,Star), [5]
                            (Column.Create, Star),
                            (Column.Forgot, Star)
                            ),
                        Children =
                        {
                            new Label()
                                .Text("User name")
                                .Row(Row.Username)
                                    .Column(0), [6]

                            new Entry()
                                .Placeholder("User name")
                                .Bind(Entry.TextProperty,
                                  nameof(LoginViewModel
                                    .Name))
                                .Row(Row.Username)
                                    .Column(1)
                                .ColumnSpan(2),
```

```
new Label()
    .Text("Password")
    .Row(Row.Password)
      .Column(0),

new Entry {IsPassword = true}
    .Placeholder("Password")
    .Bind(Entry.TextProperty,
        nameof(LoginViewModel
          .Password))
    .Row(Row.Password)
      .Column(1)
    .ColumnSpan(2),

new Button()
    .Text("Submit")
    .Row(Row.Buttons).Column
      (Column.Submit) [7]
    .Margin(5)
    .BindCommand(nameof
      (LoginViewModel
        .SubmitCommand)),
new Button()
    .Text("Create Account")
    .Margin(5)
    .Row(Row.Buttons).Column
      (Column.Create)
    .BindCommand(nameof
      (LoginViewModel
        .CreateCommand)),
new Button()
    .Margin(5)
    .Text("Forgot Password")
    .Row(Row.Buttons)
      .Column(Column.Forgot)
```

```
                                }
                            }
                        }
                };
            }
        }
```

[1] The work is done in the constructor

[2] As in the XAML, we start with `VerticalStackLayout`

[3] `Grid` is a child of `VerticalStackLayout`

[4] We define the first row to use the enumerated name and the sizing of `auto`

[5] We define the first column to use the enumerated column name and the sizing of a *star* (equivalent to 1 `*`)

[6] Notice that while the row name is meaningful and I therefore use it, the column name would not be meaningful and so I just use the offset

[7] Here, both the row name and the column name are meaningful, and it is much easier to figure out what is going on by using these names rather than the offsets

There is no doubt that `.Row(Row.Buttons).Column(Column.Create)` is much easier to understand than `Row[4].Column[1]`.

If you want to use this page, don't forget to point to your new page, `LoginCS.cs`, in `AppShell.xaml`.

> **Oops**
>
> The `Submit` button will crash the program as the `Submit` command in `LoginViewModel` is looking for `LoginPage.LoginProgressBar`. We could fix this, but the goal here was to show that you can re-write `LoginPage` in C#.

We'll stay with the original `LoginPage.xaml` for the rest of this book, as that is more complete.

ScrollView

Often, you will have more data to show than can fit on the page. This is especially frequent when working with lists, but can also be true for a form. The `ScrollView` control wraps around your other controls and allows them to be scrolled.

We saw the use of `ScrollView` in `PreferencesPage`, where we wrapped `VerticalStackLayout` in a `ScrollView` control:

```
<ScrollView>
    <VerticalStackLayout>
```

The number of preferences was just more than would show on a phone screen all at once. You can see the scroll effect a bit more if you add some more preferences to `PreferenceService`.

FlexLayout

`FlexLayout` is similar to `VerticalStackLayout` and `HorizontalStackLayout` with one crucial distinction: if you are using one of the stack layouts and the items extend past the end of the page (and you don't use `ScrollView`), anything that doesn't fit won't be rendered.

FlexLayout – seem familiar?

`FlexLayout` might be familiar if you've worked with CSS. `FlexLayout` is very similar to the Flexible Box Layout and, in fact, was based on the CSS module.

You can see the effect of `FlexLayout` by removing `ScrollView` from `PreferencesPage`. All of the remaining preferences are inaccessible.

With `FlexLayout`, the items are wrapped to the next row or column. You define which by setting the direction in `FlexLayout`. The possible directions are as follows:

- `Row`: Stacks children horizontally
- `Row-reverse`: Stacks horizontally in reverse order
- `Column`: Stacks children vertically
- `Column-reverse`: Stacks vertically in reverse order

Remove `VerticalStackLayout` and replace it with `FlexLayout`. Set the direction to `Row`:

```
<FlexLayout
    Direction="Row">
```

Figure 6.4 shows the result. It is ugly but it conveys what is happening. The excess items are wrapped horizontally.

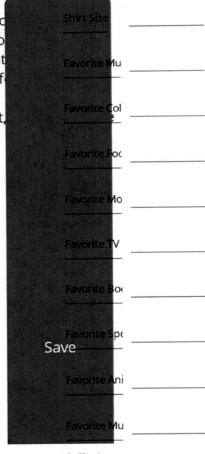

Preferences

as many preferences as you care to.

e 'free form,' fill in anything yo
:he more information you pro
better they will be able to mat
the categories can be edited f

juently as you like, and to edit,
tered and press save.

Figure 6.4 – Mangling your screen with FlexLayout

Let's see whether we can come up with a better, less ugly example.

> **Wrap**
>
> One of the properties of `FlexLayout` is `Wrap`, which defaults to *no-wrap*. Most of the time, however, you will want it to wrap, and you will end up with this wonderful syntax:
>
> ```
> Wrap = "Wrap"
> ```

We'll return to the `Login` page and, just before the end, we'll add a `HorizontalStackLayout` containing four buttons that won't quite fit, as shown in *Figure 6.5*.

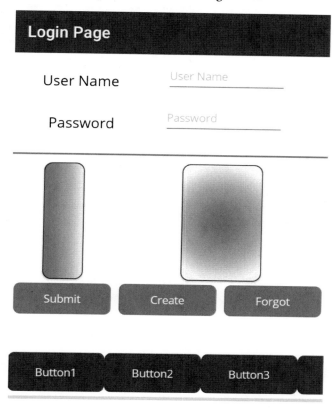

Figure 6.5 – The buttons don't fit in the row

Now, we'll replace `HorizontalStackLayout` with `FlexLayout` with `Wrap` set to `Wrap`:

```
<FlexLayout
    Direction="Row"
    Wrap="Wrap">
```

`FlexLayout` *sees* that the fourth button won't fit and wraps it to the next row, as shown in the following figure:

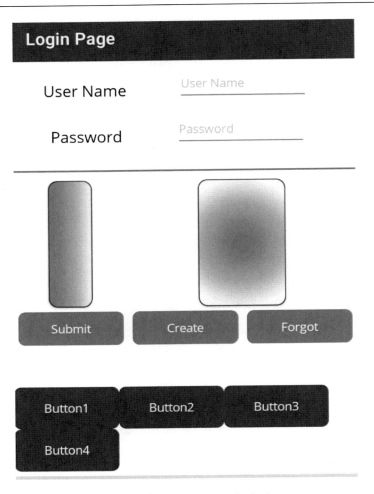

Figure 6.6 – FlexLayout wraps the buttons

.NET MAUI has added a `BindableLayout` object, which, frankly, I don't find terribly useful.

Summary

In this chapter, we looked at the principal layouts used in designing .NET MAUI apps. The most powerful and flexible of these is `Grid`, although `HorizontalStackLayout` and `VerticalStackLayout` are often used for somewhat simpler layouts.

In the next chapter, we will examine how to move from page to page and how to send data as we move. We will look at the Shell and at routing, the essential aspects of page navigation.

Quiz

1. What are the three ways you can define the width of a column in a grid?

2. If a grid's column definition looks like this – `(2*, auto, *, 100)` – how will the space be divided?

3. If a `Button` object is defined like this:

```
new Button()
    .Margin(5)
    .Text("Forgot Password")
    .Row(Row.Buttons).Column(Column.Forgot)
```

   What do we know about its position?

4. What is the advantage of `Grid` over using `VerticalStackLayout` and `HorizontalStackLayout`?

5. Why is `BindableLayout` less useful than, for example, `CollectionView`?

You try it

Create a page that looks like a standard four-function calculator. Use the layout shown in *Figure 6.7*. Extra credit: implement the functionality and display the result in a `Label`.

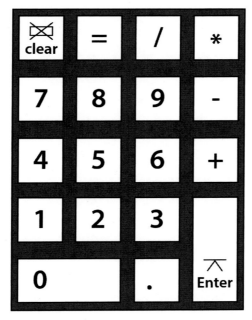

Figure 6.7 – Four-function calculator

Part 2 – Intermediate Topics

With the basics under our belt, we'll go on to look at a number of intermediate topics, including how you navigate from one page to the next and how you store data, both for a user's preferences and in a relational database. We'll end with the most important topic – creating unit tests.

This part has the following chapters:

- *Chapter 7, Understanding Navigation*
- *Chapter 8, Storing and Retrieving Data*
- *Chapter 9, Unit Testing*

Understanding Navigation

Until now, we've been working with one page at a time, with no way to get to a page except by setting it in AppShell.xaml. Of course, this will not do for a real application, so in this chapter, we'll look at various options for navigating from page to page. As you'll see, .NET MAUI uses *shell navigation*, a process we'll look at in some depth.

This chapter includes the following topics:

- Exploring the TabBar
- Creating the About and Buddies pages
- Shell navigation
- Routing
- Passing values from page to page

Technical requirements

To get the most out of this chapter, you'll need a copy of Visual Studio. The source code for the completed code shown in this chapter can be found here: `https://github.com/PacktPublishing/. NET-MAUI-for-C-Sharp-Developers/tree/Navigation`. If you want to follow along, start with the code from the completion of *Chapter 6*.

Exploring the TabBar

ForgetMeNot's principal form of navigation will be the `TabBar control`. A Tab Bar is a way to jump to a specific page without going through other pages. It consists of icons, and sometimes descriptive text, across the bottom of every page, as shown in the following screenshot:

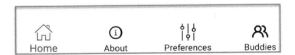

Figure 7.1 – Tab Bar in the completed project

The four tabs at the bottom, as shown in *Figure 7.1*, will take the user directly to the respective page.

> **The Home page**
>
> Here you see the tabs we created on `MainPage,` which we created in *Chapter 4*, one of which we've titled **Home**.

You create `TabBar` in `AppShell.xaml`. Within the `TabBar` tags, you provide one `ShellContent` element for each page. `ShellContent` has a `Title` property (the text displayed), an `Icon` property (the image displayed), and `ContentTemplate`, which specifies the content for this tab:

```xaml
<TabBar >
    <ShellContent
        Title="Home"
        ContentTemplate="{DataTemplate view:MainPage}"
        Icon="icon_home" />

    <ShellContent
        Title="About"
        ContentTemplate="{DataTemplate view:About}"
        Icon="icon_about" />

    <ShellContent
        Title="Preferences"
        ContentTemplate="{DataTemplate view:Preferences}"
        Icon="icon_prefs" />

    <ShellContent
        Title="Buddies"
        ContentTemplate="{DataTemplate view:BuddyList}"
        Icon="icon_buddies" />
</TabBar>
```

Next, we need to create the pages that each `ContentTemplate` points to so that we can see `TabBar` at work.

Creating the About and Buddies pages

To see this navigation work, you'll need to add the missing pages: **About** and **Buddies**. Creating the **About** page is very straightforward. Right-click on the **View** folder and choose **Add New Item**. If needed, expand the **AddNewItem** dialog.

From the left panel, choose **.NET MAUI** and on the right, choose **.NET MAUI ContentPage (XAML)**. At the bottom of the dialog, put in the name for the new page: `AboutPage.xaml`, as shown in *Figure 7.2*:

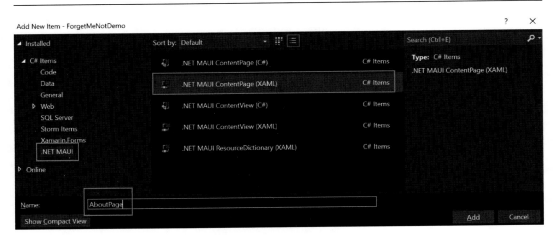

Figure 7.2 – Creating AboutPage

The **About** page is very simple and does not require any new types of controls.

Assembling the About page

Let's assemble the **About** page quickly, as there is nothing new here. We'll need the XAML to display the current version, and so on, and we'll need the code-behind file to establish `BindingContext`. Finally, we'll need `ViewModel`. Eventually, the **About** page will ask the service for its version number, but for now, we'll hardcode that:

```xml
<?xml version="1.0" encoding="utf-8" ?>
<ContentPage xmlns="http://schemas.microsoft.com/dotnet/
   2021/maui"
    xmlns:x="http://schemas.microsoft.com/winfx/2009/xaml"
            x:Class="ForgetMeNotDemo.View.AboutPage"
            Title="About">
    <VerticalStackLayout Margin="10" Spacing="10">
        <HorizontalStackLayout Spacing="10">
            <Label
                FontAttributes="Bold"
                FontSize="22"
                Text="About this app"
                VerticalOptions="End" />
            <Label
                FontSize="22"
                Text="v0.1"
```

```
                    VerticalOptions="End" />
            </HorizontalStackLayout>

            <HorizontalStackLayout Spacing="10">
                <Label
                    FontAttributes="Bold"
                    FontSize="22"
                    Text="Api Version"
                    VerticalOptions="End" />
                <Label
                    FontSize="22"
                    Text="{Binding ApiVersion}"
                    VerticalOptions="End" />
            </HorizontalStackLayout>

            <Label
                HeightRequest="60"
                Text="This app is written in XAML and C# with
                    .NET MAUI by Jesse Liberty and Rodrigo Juarez."
                VerticalTextAlignment="Center" />
            <Label
                HeightRequest="60"
                Text="Concept and original design by Robin
                    Liberty"
                VerticalTextAlignment="Center" />
            <Label FontSize="Small" Text="Icons from IconScout:
                https://iconscout.com" />
        </VerticalStackLayout>
    </ContentPage>
```

The code-behind file looks like this (for now):

```
public AboutPage()
{
    BindingContext = new AboutViewModel();
    InitializeComponent();
}
```

And, finally, `ViewModel` looks like this (for now):

```
namespace ForgetMeNotDemo.ViewModel;


[ObservableObject]
public partial class AboutViewModel
{

    [ObservableProperty] private string apiVersion;

    public AboutViewModel()
    {
        apiVersion = "1.0";
    }


}
```

The **About** page currently looks like this:

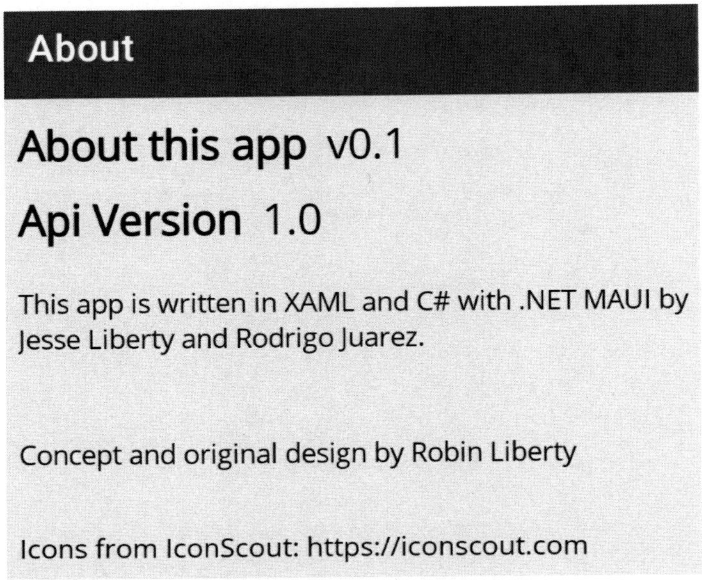

Figure 7.3 – The About page

That will give us something to work with.

Next, we need a **BuddiesPage**, that is, a page that lists all the user's friends and relatives. Each Buddy will have a list of **preferences** that we can use when it is time to buy them a present.

For now, we'll just use the out-of-the-box page that we get when we right-click on **View** and add a new **.NET MAUI XAML** page, as shown in *Figure 7.4*:

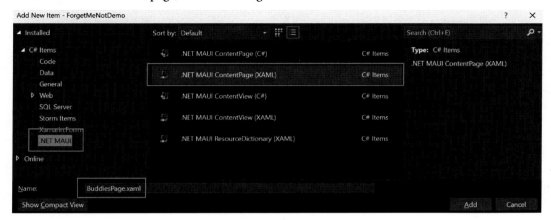

Figure 7.4 – Creating the Buddies page

Next, open `BuddiesPage.xaml` and make one small change. Where the `Text` field of the `Label` control says, `Welcome to .NET MAUI!` change it to `Buddies Page` so that we'll know where we are when we navigate there. If you want, add a space between the words in the title as well:

```xml
<?xml version="1.0" encoding="utf-8" ?>
<ContentPage xmlns="http://schemas.microsoft.com/dotnet/
    2021/maui"
        xmlns:x="http://schemas.microsoft.com/winfx/2009/xaml"
            x:Class="ForgetMeNotDemo.View.BuddiesPage"
            Title="Buddies Page">
    <VerticalStackLayout>
        <Label
            Text="Buddies Page"
            VerticalOptions="Center"
            HorizontalOptions="Center" />
    </VerticalStackLayout>
</ContentPage>
```

Next, create `BuddiesViewModel` by right-clicking on the **ViewModel** folder and choosing **Add | Class**.

Finally, we need to tell the app where to start. We'll do that in App.xaml.cs where we will set MainPage to be the new AppShell (which is how we'll kick off the program and set ourselves up for shell navigation as described):

```
namespace ForgetMeNotDemo;

public partial class App : Application
{

public App()

{



InitializeComponent();



MainPage = new AppShell();

}
}
```

Here is what AppShell.xaml should look like now:

```
<?xml version="1.0" encoding="UTF-8" ?>
<Shell
    Shell.FlyoutBehavior="Disabled"
    x:Class="ForgetMeNotDemo.AppShell"
    xmlns="http://schemas.microsoft.com/dotnet/2021/maui"
    xmlns:local="clr-namespace:ForgetMeNotDemo"
    xmlns:view="clr-namespace:ForgetMeNotDemo.View"
    xmlns:x="http://schemas.microsoft.com/winfx/2009/xaml">

    <TabBar>
        <ShellContent
            Title="Home"
            ContentTemplate="{DataTemplate view:MainPage}"
```

```
        Icon="icon_home" />

    <ShellContent
        Title="About"
        ContentTemplate="{DataTemplate view:AboutPage}"
        Icon="icon_about" />

    <ShellContent
        Title="Preferences"
        ContentTemplate="{DataTemplate
          view:PreferencesPage}"
        Icon="icon_prefs" />

    <ShellContent
        Title="Buddies"
        ContentTemplate="{DataTemplate
          view:BuddiesPage}"
        Icon="icon_buddies" />
    </TabBar>


</Shell>
```

One more thing. Notice that each tab has an icon. To make that work and look as intended, you'll either need to find icons online or get them by checking out the source code for this chapter in the Navigation branch.

In either case, simply copy the images to the resources\image folder of your project, replacing the three dots with the full path on your computer.

Image support

Those of you who have worked with Xamarin.Forms will be delighted to know that the days of creating different size images and distributing them to the various folders for both iOS and Android are now over. Put the .svg file into the images folder and .NET MAUI will do all the rest for you! (You can use a .png file, but it won't scale as nicely. To make the point, I made our flower image a .png file.)

Run the application and click on the various tabs. You should see it navigating to the various pages we've created. Notice in *Figure 7.5* that the current tab *lights up* – you get the effect for free and you do not have to create two icons, one for each of the currently selected and not selected icons.

Figure 7.5 – The Home tab "lit up"

Now that our tabs and pages are in place, it is time to look at how you move from one page to another when there aren't tabs for the pages you want to navigate to.

Shell navigation

That would be all you need to know about navigation if your app was just going to have the four pages that we're accessing by the TabBar. Of course, you'll almost certainly have more pages than that, and you'll want a way to navigate from one page to another.

To see navigation from one page to another without using TabBar, we'll need another page to navigate to. Let's create the **BuddyDetailsPage**, which we'll navigate to from the **Buddies** page.

Once again, take the out-of-the-box page, but change Label to say Buddy Details Page:

```xml
<?xml version="1.0" encoding="utf-8" ?>
<ContentPage xmlns="http://schemas.microsoft.com/dotnet/
   2021/maui"
      xmlns:x="http://schemas.microsoft.com/winfx/2009/xaml"
         x:Class="ForgetMeNotDemo.View.BuddyDetailsPage"
            Title="Buddy Details Page">
      <VerticalStackLayout>
         <Label
            Text="Buddy Details Page"
            VerticalOptions="Center"
            HorizontalOptions="Center" />
      </VerticalStackLayout>
</ContentPage>
```

Next, return to the **Buddies** page, add a Button that says Go to details and give it the GoToDetailsCommand command:

```xml
<Button Text="Go to details"
      Command="{Binding GoToDetailsCommand}" />
```

In the **BuddiesViewModel** page, we'll need to handle the GoToDetails command. The goal of our handler will be to navigate to **BuddyDetails**. We do that with *shell navigation*. Here's the code to do so:

```csharp
[RelayCommand]
private async Task GoToDetails()
{
   await Shell.Current.GoToAsync("buddydetailspage");
}
```

> **BindingContext**
> Remember that for the `GoToDetails` command to work, you must bind the XAML to `ViewModel` by setting `BindingContext` in the code-behind file.

In this common construct, you pass in the page name to the `GoToAsync` static method on `Shell.Current`. The key question is, *how does it know what buddydetailspage is, given that buddydetailspage is a string?* The answer to that lies in *routing*, which we'll cover next.

Routing

In .NET MAUI, you register your routes in `AppShell.xaml.cs`. For example, to connect the `buddydetailspage` string to the actual `BuddyDetailsPage`, you would add this:

```
Routing.RegisterRoute("buddydetailspage",
  typeof(BuddyDetailsPage));
```

We'll create a routing entry for all of the pages, including the ones we can access through tabs. This will give us the greatest flexibility:

```
public partial class AppShell : Shell
{
  public AppShell()
  {
    InitializeComponent();

    Routing.RegisterRoute("buddiespage",
      typeof(BuddiesPage));
    Routing.RegisterRoute("buddydetailspage",
      typeof(BuddyDetailsPage));
    Routing.RegisterRoute("aboutpage", typeof(AboutPage));
    Routing.RegisterRoute("preferencespage",
      typeof(PreferencesPage));
    Routing.RegisterRoute("loginpage", typeof(LoginPage));
    Routing.RegisterRoute("mainpage", typeof(MainPage));
  }

}
```

Now the routing works as if by magic. You tell it where you want to go, passing in the route, and .NET MAUI handles the navigation. Start up the program if it isn't already running and tap on the **Buddies** tab. On the **Buddies** page, tap on the **Details** button, and hey presto! You should be on the **Buddy Details** page. Easy peasy.

It's great to be able to move from one page to another, but often the first page has data that the second page needs. So, let's look at how you send that data to the second page.

Passing values from page to page

When navigating from one page to another, you'll often want to pass in a value. There are a few ways to do this; here are the two most common:

1. Using the url (?) syntax as you might with a URL to navigate to a page on the web
2. Using navigation parameters with a dictionary

Passing values with the url (?) syntax

Let's return to the Buddies page. Right now, the Button has a GoToDetailsCommand command. But the **Details** page needs to know which Buddy to show details about.

We'll modify RelayCommand in ViewModel to pass in BuddyId. To make this work, we need a Buddy object (which will have the Id). However, Buddy is just one of the types of users of this program, so let's start by defining the User type:

```
[ObservableObject]
public partial class User
{
    [ObservableProperty]
    private string name;

    [ObservableProperty]    [1]
    private string id;

    [ObservableProperty]
    private List<Buddy> buddies;    [2]

    [ObservableProperty]
//    private List<Invitation> invitations; [3]

    [ObservableProperty]
```

```
    private List<Preference> preferences; [4]


}
```

[1] Here is the `Id` property we'll need.

[2] A user may have a collection of `buddies` (we'll come back to this).

[3] A user may have a collection of `invitations`, which are sent out to potential `buddies` (we'll come back to this too).

[4] The user has a list of `preference` objects, as we've seen earlier.

The Buddy class derives from the `User` class. Here it is in full, though we won't be using most of these properties for now:

```
public partial class Buddy : User
{
    [ObservableProperty] private string emailAddress;
    [ObservableProperty] private string? phoneNumber;
    [ObservableProperty] private string?
      mailingAddressLine1;
    [ObservableProperty] private string?
      mailingAddressLine2;
    [ObservableProperty] private string? website;
    [ObservableProperty] private string? twitter;
    [ObservableProperty] private string? facebook;
    [ObservableProperty] private string? instagram;
    [ObservableProperty] private string? linkedIn;
    [ObservableProperty] private string? venmoName;
    [ObservableProperty] private DateTime buddySince;


}
```

> **Inheriting ObservableObject**
>
> Notice that Buddy is not marked with the `ObservableObject` attribute. That is because it inherits from `User`, which is marked as `ObservableObject`.

We will want to give the new page the Id of the Buddy object we're passing in. We can do that using either of the methods for passing data (for example, the URL approach or the dictionary).

Passing the Buddy Id

Returning to the **Buddies** page, there are two ways to get Id to the **BuddiesDetail** page. The first is just to pass Id using the ? syntax:

```
private async Task GoToDetails()
{
   await Shell.Current.GoToAsync
     ($"buddydetailspage?id={Id}");


}
```

If you want to pass two properties, for example, Id and Name, you concatenate them with &&. This should all be familiar to you from URLs you might use in a browser:

```
private async Task GoToDetails()
{
   await Shell.Current.GoToAsync
     ($"buddydetailspage?id={Id}&&name={"BuddyName"});


}
```

This won't work if we don't have Id and Name in BuddiesViewModel, so let's add that here:

```
public partial class BuddiesViewModel
{
   [ObservableProperty] private string id = "001";
   [ObservableProperty] private string name = "jesse";
```

The call to GoToAsync will change pages to BuddyDetailsPage and send the parameters to the associated ViewModel (BuddyDetailsViewModel).

QueryProperty

We mark up the receiving ViewModel with the QueryProperty attribute along with the name of the property to associate it with ViewModel and the string used in the GoToAsync method.

To make that clearer, let's create BuddyDetailsViewModel, and mark it as ObservableObject. We'll give it two properties: Id and Name:

```
[ObservableObject]
public partial class BuddyDetailsViewModel
{
    [ObservableProperty] private string id;
    [ObservableProperty] private string name;
}
```

We want the first parameter we passed in (id) to be assigned to the Id property, and we want the second parameter we passed in to be assigned to the Name property. For that, we use the QueryProperty attribute (placed above the class):

```
using CommunityToolkit.Mvvm.ComponentModel;

namespace ForgetMeNotDemo.ViewModel;

[ObservableObject]
[QueryProperty(nameof(Id), "id")]
[QueryProperty(nameof(Name), "buddyname")]

public partial class BuddyDetailsViewModel
{

    [ObservableProperty] private string id;
    [ObservableProperty] private string name;
}
```

Now that you are comfortable with the two ways to pass data, let's take a look at how we can integrate that into the flow of the program.

Putting it together

On the **Buddies** page, the user clicks on **GoToDetails**.

This fires the GoToDetails relay command in BuddiesViewModel.

That method calls the following:

```
await Shell.Current.GoToAsync
    ($"buddydetailspage?id={{Id}}&&buddyname={{Name}}");
```

This call to `GoToAsync` transfers us to `BuddyDetailsPage`, but passes in the two parameters (`Id` and `Name`) to `BuddyDetailsViewModel`!

`BuddyDetailsViewModel` parses the `QueryProperty` attributes and distributes the values to the associated properties.

The net effect is that you are now on `BuddyDetailsPage` with the `Id` and `Name` properties in the associated `ViewModel` populated with values.

To see this at work, go to the `BuddyDetailsPage.xaml` file and add two Label controls, one bound to `Id` and the other to `Name`.

Here's the XAML page:

```xml
<?xml version="1.0" encoding="utf-8" ?>
<ContentPage
    Title="Buddy Details Page"
    x:Class="ForgetMeNotDemo.View.BuddyDetailsPage"
    xmlns="http://schemas.microsoft.com/dotnet/2021/maui"
    xmlns:x="http://schemas.microsoft.com/winfx/2009/xaml">
    <VerticalStackLayout>
        <Label
            HorizontalOptions="Center"
            Text="Buddy Details Page"
            VerticalOptions="Center" />
        <Label Text="{Binding Id}"/>
        <Label Text="{Binding Name}"/>
    </VerticalStackLayout>
</ContentPage>
```

Remember to set `BindingContext` in the code-behind page.

Run the program and click on the **Buddies** tab. On the **Buddies** page, click on **GoToDetails** You will be transferred to the **BuddiesDetails** page, and the two values will be displayed.

> **Stop right there**
> Make sure you understand how all this hangs together before going ahead. If necessary, re-read starting with the *Passing values from page to page* section.

Passing values with a dictionary

At times, you will want to pass an entire object (or more) to the receiving `ViewModel`. You do this by instantiating a dictionary where the key is a string, and the value is an object.

Let's revise `GoToDetails` to take an entire `Buddy` object. First, we need to create a `Buddy` object and put it into `BuddyViewModel`:

```
[ObservableProperty] private Buddy rodrigo = new Buddy
{
  Id = "002",
  Name = "Rodrigo Juarez",
  Website = "https://jesseliberty.com"
};
```

Next, we need to create our dictionary. We can pick any arbitrary string as the key, and pass in the `Buddy` object (`rodrigo`) that we just created:

```
[RelayCommand]
private async Task GoToDetails()
{
  var navigationParameter = new Dictionary<string, object>
  {
    {"TheBuddy", Rodrigo}
  };

  await Shell.Current.GoToAsync($"buddydetailspage",
    navigationParameter);
}
```

Once again, we are redirected to the **BuddyDetails Page** (based on the routing) but this time, the Buddy object itself is passed in. At the top of the **BuddyDetailsPage,** we indicate which Buddy object field to assign the incoming Buddy to, and we use the key from the dictionary:

```
[ObservableObject]
[QueryProperty(nameof(MyBuddy), "TheBuddy")]
public partial class BuddyDetailsViewModel
{
```

We'll add three properties for the page to bind to:

```
[ObservableProperty] private string id;
[ObservableProperty] private string name;
[ObservableProperty] private string? website;
```

Notice that `website` is a nullable string. This is because it is marked as `nullable` in the Buddy definition. To make this work, you'll want to enable `nullable`, at least on this page if not for the project.

The easiest way to manage the incoming Buddy object is as follows:

```
private Buddy myBuddy;

public Buddy MyBuddy
{
  get => myBuddy;
  set
  {
    Id = value.Id;
    Name = value.Name;
    Website = value.Website;
  }
}
```

If you go to `BuddyDetailsPage.xaml` and add a label whose text binds to `website`, the result will be as shown in *Figure 7.5*:

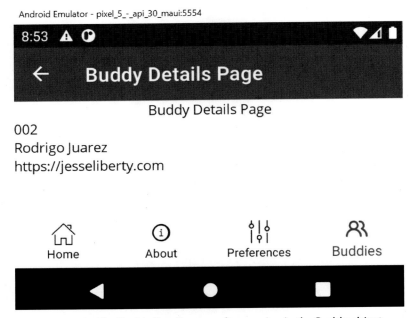

Figure 7.6 – The Buddy Details page after passing in the Buddy object

Putting it together

This can, at first, be confusing enough that it is worth going through the flow step by step.

In BuddiesPage, the user clicks on **GoToDetails** This fires GoToDetailsCommand, which is handled in BuddiesViewModel.

In ViewModel, we have a Buddy property (as defined in the Models folder). The identifier for that Buddy object is rodrigo, and three of its fields are initialized.

We then assemble a dictionary to use as the parameter to the GoToAsync method. We pass in the name of the page we want to navigate to (as recorded in the AppShell.xaml.cs file in the Routing.RegisterRoute method).

We also pass in the dictionary we just created.

.NET MAUI navigates to the page, and our dictionary is routed to the associated ViewModel (BuddyDetailsViewModel). There, the QueryProperty attribute associates the MyBuddy property with queryid, which we used in BuddiesPage.

The property it matches is a Buddy type, so we can set the local properties with the properties from the Buddy object passed in (value).

Since BuddyDetailsPage has Labels that bind to these properties in ViewModel, the right things are displayed.

Summary

In this chapter, we have focused on how you can move from one page to another without using `TabBar`, by using shell navigation and routesinstead.. We also looked at how you can pass data from the first page to the second using either URL syntax or by passing a dictionary containing the object or values you want to send.

In the next chapter, we will examine storing and retrieving data.

Quiz

1. Where do you define `TabBar`?
2. What are the three properties of `TabBar ShellContent`?
3. Where are routes registered?
4. What is the method for navigating to another page?
5. What are the ways we've seen to pass data to a page?

You try it

Modify `RelayCommand Submit` in `LoginViewModel` to display the progress bar and then navigate to the **Buddies** page. Pass in the username and password, first as strings, then as a dictionary. Temporarily modify the **Buddies** page to display the values passed in.

8
Storing and Retrieving Data

You now have all the fundamentals to create and navigate pages, layouts, and the controls used to populate pages. Congratulations! You are now a .NET MAUI programmer.

This chapter begins the intermediate section of the book, in which you will see how to store and retrieve data and then create unit tests – both critical aspects of writing real-world and, especially, enterprise apps.

Programs interact with data, and most need to store that data after an app closes and restore it as needed when the app resumes. In this chapter, we will consider two variations on this – long-term persistence of user preferences and long-term database storage.

We will cover the following topics in this chapter:

- Storing user preferences
- Storing to a database on your device

Technical requirements

To follow along with this chapter, you will need Visual Studio. You will also install another `NuGet` package, as shown later in this chapter.

The source code for the finished code in this chapter can be found here: `https://github.com/PacktPublishing/.NET-MAUI-for-C-Sharp-Developers/tree/persistence`. To follow along, you will need to use the code from the previous chapter.

Storing user preferences

Most apps allow a user to set preferences that can be stored on a phone and retrieved, typically when the app starts. .NET MAUI provides a service for this, easily storing *key/value pairs*, such as theme preferences, the last date used, the login name, and so on.

.NET MAUI provides the `IPreferences` interface to help store these preferences. With this, and the associated `Preferences` class (both in the `Microsoft.Maui.Storage` namespace), you can store string keys and values of any of the following types:

- `Boolean`
- `Double`
- `Int` (`int32`, `single`, and `int64`)
- `String`
- `DateTime`

Persisting DateTime

`DateTime` values are stored as 64-bit integers and use the `ToBinary` and `FromBinary` methods to encode and decode respectively.

Let's create a `UserPreferences` page with a short form to gather a user's preferences. We'll also add `Button`, which will display all the saved preferences and allow the user to delete one or all of them.

Name collisions

We have a preferences page, which may cause a problem because we want to use the built-in `Preferences` object. To solve this, go to `PreferencesViewModel` and rename `List<Preference> preferenceList`. There should be no other conflicts. The safest way to rename is to use the Visual Studio rename functionality, which you can get to by putting your cursor on the name and entering `Control-R R`. After you rename, you may have to manually rename `ObservableProperties`, depending on the latest update to Visual Studio.

The new `UserPreferences` page will gather three preferences from the user, which are as follows:

- The user's display name
- The preferred theme
- Whether the app can be used on cellular or Wi-Fi only

Light and dark themes

It has become common in apps to offer a user light and dark themes. In .NET MAUI, you can offer the user the choice, or if you are ambitious, you can create your own themes.

We will gather but not implement a user's preferences relating to light and dark themes.

Here is the `UserPreferences` page:

```xml
<?xml version="1.0" encoding="utf-8" ?>
<ContentPage
    Title="User Preferences"
    x:Class="ForgetMeNotDemo.View.UserPreferencesPage"
    xmlns="http://schemas.microsoft.com/dotnet/2021/maui"
    xmlns:x="http://schemas.microsoft.com/winfx/2009/xaml">
    <VerticalStackLayout>
        <Grid
            ColumnDefinitions="*,*"
            RowDefinitions="*,*,*,*">
            <Label
                Grid.Column="0"
                Grid.Row="0"
                Text="Display Name" />
            <Entry
                Grid.Column="1"
                Grid.Row="0"
                Placeholder="Your name as you want it
                    displayed"
                Text="{Binding DisplayName}" />
```

Having gathered the user's display name, we can go on to ask them which of the two mutually exclusive themes they'd like. To do so, we will use `RadioButtonGroup` and two `RadioButtons`, initializing `Light` to be selected:

```xml
            <Label
                Grid.Column="0"
                Grid.Row="1"
                Text="Theme" />
            <HorizontalStackLayout
                Grid.Column="1"
                Grid.Row="1"
                RadioButtonGroup.GroupName="{Binding
                    ThemeGroupName}" [1]
                RadioButtonGroup.SelectedValue="{Binding
                    ThemeSelection}"> [2]
```

```
                <RadioButton Content="Dark" />
                <RadioButton
                    Content="Light"
                    IsChecked="True" /> [3]
            </HorizontalStackLayout>
```

We now want to ask the user whether the app should only be used when connected to Wi-Fi. We can do this with a switch control, where on indicates `WiFi only` is `true`:

```
            <Label
                Grid.Column="0"
                Grid.Row="2"
                Text="Wifi Only?" />
            <Switch                    [4]
                Grid.Column="1"
                Grid.Row="2"
                HorizontalOptions="Start"
                IsToggled="{Binding WifiOnly}"
                OnColor="Green"
                ThumbColor="Blue" />
            <Button
                Command="{Binding SavePreferencesCommand}"
                Grid.Column="0"
                Grid.ColumnSpan="2"
                Grid.Row="3"
                HorizontalOptions="Center"
                Text="Save" />
        </Grid>
    </VerticalStackLayout>
</ContentPage>
```

[1] Here, we introduce a new control, `RadioButton`. Radio buttons are in either implicit or explicit groups. Implicit groups are created by putting all the `RadioButtons` into the same container (for example, `VerticalStackLayout`). Explicit groups are given `GroupName`, as we see here.

[2] The user's choice is recorded by the `SelectedValue` property.

[3] When defining `RadioButtons`, you can (and should) set exactly one to `IsChecked=true`.

[4] The switch control toggles off and on (`false` and `true`).

Now that we know how to gather the information the user wants to save, let's take a look at the lightweight mechanism provided by .NET MAUI to do so.

UserPreferencesViewModel

As you might expect, the first thing we'll do is create properties for the bound controls:

```
[ObservableObject]
public partial class UserPreferencesViewModel
{
    [ObservableProperty] private string displayName;
    [ObservableProperty] private string themeSelection;
    [ObservableProperty] private bool wifiOnly;
    public string ThemeGroupName => "Theme";
```

Next, we need to handle the `SavePreferences` command. We do this using the .NET MAUI `Preferences` object, calling the static `Set` method:

```
[RelayCommand]
public async Task SavePreferences()
{
    Preferences.Default.Set("DisplayName", displayName);
    Preferences.Default.Set("ThemeSelection",
        themeSelection);
    Preferences.Default.Set("WifiOnly", wifiOnly);
}
```

.NET MAUI will handle the persistence for us.

Now that we've created the page, let's set up navigation to get to it.

Navigating to UserPreferences

We need a way to get to our new page. A typical place to put this would be an **About** page. Let's add `Button` as the last item in `VerticalStackLayout`:

```
<Button
    Command="{Binding OpenPreferencesCommand}"
    Text="Preferences"
    WidthRequest="150"
    Margin="10,50,10,0"/>
```

The OnPreferences command simply navigates to our new page:

```
[RelayCommand]
public async Task OpenPreferences()
{
  await Shell.Current.GoToAsync("userpreferences");


}
```

Make sure you register the userpreferences page in AppShell before invoking this method.

The page isn't pretty, but it is ready to gather a user's preferences, as shown in the following figure:

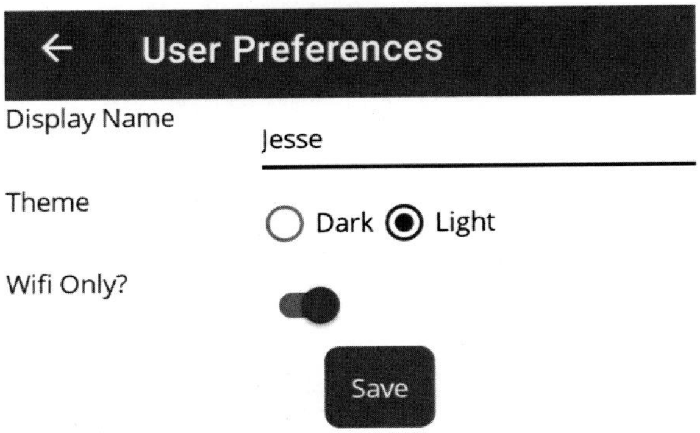

Figure 8.1 – The preferences page

A user is now able to set their preferences. The next time they start up the app, we'll want to retrieve those preferences and set the app accordingly.

Retrieving the preferences

When a user closes the app, the preferences are preserved. The next time we return to the preferences page, we should see the preferences restored. We accomplish this using the Get method on Preferences. Default.

The Get method takes two parameters, the *key* and *a default value*. We'll put this in the ViewModel constructor so that the preferences page is populated when it is displayed:

```
public UserPreferencesViewModel()
{
  displayName = Preferences.Default.Get("DisplayName",
    "Unknown");
```

```
    themeSelection = Preferences.Default.Get
      ("ThemeSelection", "Light");
  wifiOnly = Preferences.Default.Get("WifiOnly", false);
}
```

Note that the first argument to Get is the key, as defined in the Set method in the SavePreferences method. The second argument is the default value that will be provided if the key is not present.

Checking for a key

While you don't have to check that a key exists before trying to retrieve it, there are times when you'll want to differentiate between the value you get back being the default value or the value that is actually stored (for example, is WiFiOnly false because it really is false, or because that key doesn't exist and you received the default value?).

To manage this, you can use the ContainsKey method on Preferences.Default:

```
bool knowsWifi = Preferences.DefaultContainsKey("WifiOnly");
```

The user can now store their preferences, and in theory, they can be restored. Let's make sure that this is working.

Testing the persistence

To see that this works, navigate to the UserPreferences page by way of the **About** page, and fill in the three preferences. Then, stop the program and restart it. When you return to the UserPreferences page, you should see that your entered values have been restored.

Clear

If you want to clear a specific UserPreference, use the Remove method:

```
Preferences.Default.Remove("DisplayName");
```

To remove them all, use the Clear method:

```
Preferences.Default.Clear()
```

The Preferences interface is designed to hold simple data in key/value pairs. Microsoft warns against storing long strings, as it may negatively affect performance. If you need to store more complex or larger data, you'll want to use a database, and the database of choice for many .NET MAUI developers is **SQLite**.

The lightweight persistence mechanism is great for storing relatively short strings and other primitives, but if you are going to store substantial data, you'll need a real database.

Storing to a database on your device

There are a couple of contenders for storing data on your device. The most popular is SQLite, which is an open source, small, fast, and highly reliable database. It is the most used database in the world and is built into all mobile phones and most computers.

Installing SQLite

To get started, install the latest version of the **sqlite-net-pcl** NuGet package, as shown in *Figure 8.2*.

Figure 8.2 – Installing sqlite-net-pcl

> **Installing the correct package**
>
> There are a number of SQLite packages available on NuGet. The one you want is **sqlite-net-pcl** and has the author **SQLite-net**, as shown in *Figure 8.3*.

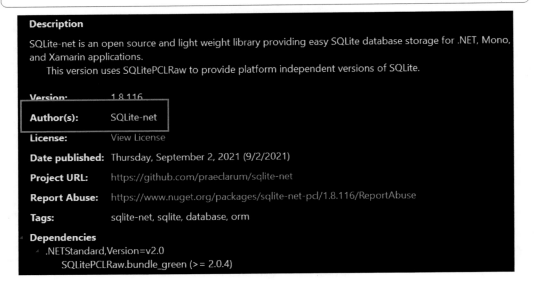

Figure 8.3 – The author should be SQLite-net

Once **sqlite-net-pcl** is installed, also search for `sqlitepclraw.bundle_green` and if it is not automatically installed, manually install **SQLitePCLRaw.bundle_green**, as shown in *Figure 8.4*.

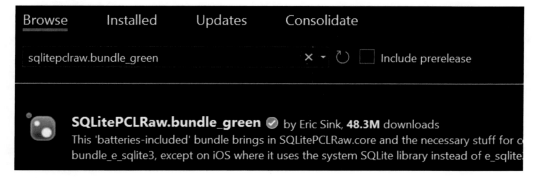

Figure 8.4 – Installing SQLitePCLRaw.bundle_green

With the packages installed, you are ready to set up your program to create and use an SQLite database.

Getting started with SQLite

To create your database, you'll need to store the database filename and its path among other constant values. To do so, right-click on your project and create a `Constants.cs` file. For convenience, I'll create a `Database` folder and place it there:

```
namespace ForgetMeNotDemo.Database;
public static class Constants
{
  public const string DatabaseFilename =
    "ForgetMeNotDemo.db3"; [1]

  public const SQLite.SQLiteOpenFlags Flags = [2]
    SQLite.SQLiteOpenFlags.ReadWrite |
    SQLite.SQLiteOpenFlags.Create |
    SQLite.SQLiteOpenFlags.SharedCache;

  public static string DatabasePath =>
    Path.Combine(FileSystem.AppDataDirectory,
      DatabaseFilename); [3]
}
```

[1] Set the name for your database. Feel free to use the name as shown or rename it to whatever you like.

[2] Set the flags for how the file should be managed. Here, we've set it to read/write mode, to create the database if it doesn't exist, and finally, to enable multithreaded database access.

[3] Append the database filename we created earlier to the directory name for the app.

With these constants established, we're ready to create the database. We'll encapsulate that work in a class.

The Database class

It is a common pattern to wrap a database access layer in a class, abstracting it away and decoupling it from the rest of the app. We'll put all the query logic into this class. This centralization of database concerns will help make our app scalable over time.

The class will need an Init() method to create the database and our first table. To get us started, let's create a table to hold all our preferences:

```
using ForgetMeNotDemo.Database;
using ForgetMeNotDemo.Model;
using SQLite;
namespace ForetMeNotDemoDatabase;
public class ForgetMeNotDemoDatabase
{
    private SQLiteAsyncConnection Database;    [1]

    private async Task Init()
    {
        if (Database is not null)    [2]
            return;

        Database = new SQLiteAsyncConnection(    [3]
            Constants.DatabasePath,
            Constants.Flags);
        await Database.CreateTableAsync<Preference>(); [4]
    }
}
```

[1] Declare an object of type SQLiteAsyncConnection and name it Database.

[2] If it already exists, then return (that is, treat it as a singleton).

[3] Create `SQliteAsyncConnection`, passing in the path and flags from the `constant` class.

[4] Create our first table, declaring the type of object we'll store in the table (the `Preference` objects).

We are ready to start using the database, to add and manipulate our table.

CRUD

As is true for virtually all databases, we'll want to support **Create, Read, Update, and Delete (CRUD)**. For now, let's just implement the methods to create and read records. The method to create is typically combined with the update method.

Create/update

We're going to want to know whether a `Preference` is already in the table so that we know, when given a `Preference` record, whether to add it or update it. It will need a unique ID. Fortunately, SQLite is very good at providing IDs.

Start by opening `Preference.cs` in the `Model` folder and adding an `id` property:

```
[ObservableObject]
public partial class Preference
{
    [ObservableProperty] private int id;
    [ObservableProperty] private string preferencePrompt;
    [ObservableProperty] private string preferenceValue;


}
```

Next, return to `ForgetMeNotDemoDatabase.cs` and add the `SavePreference` method:

```
public async Task<int> SavePreference(Preference
    preference) [1]
{
    await Init();   [2]
    if (preference.Id != 0) [3]
    {
        return await Database.UpdateAsync(preference);
    }
    else
    {
        return await Database.InsertAsync(preference);
```

```
        }
    }
```

[1] Our `SavePreference` method takes the type (`Preference`) as an argument and returns the number of rows updated (in this case, zero or one).

[2] Call `Init` on the database each time you take an action.

[3] Check to see whether the `Preference` object has `Id`. Since `Id` is an `int` type, it defaults to zero, so if it is not zero, we need to do an update; otherwise, we need to do an insert.

Now that we can create (or update) a record, let's write code to read that data out of the database.

Read

We'll want to be able to get all our preferences back from the database. For that, we'll create a `GetPreferences` method that returns a list of `Preference` objects:

```
public async Task<List<Preference>> GetPreferences()
{
    await Init();
    return await Database.Table<Preference>();
}
```

> **Soft deletion**
>
> When we write our `Delete` method, we probably will want to do a *soft* deletion – that is, mark it as deleted rather than actually removing it. For this to work, you'll need to add another property to `Preference`, `Deleted`, and also `int`. Our read statement will then take a `where` clause, checking that the `Deleted` property is equal to zero.

Once you have a database design, you need to decide whether you are going to keep the database locally on a device or in the cloud, accessed through your API.

Local or remote?

A design question for this app is whether we want to store our preferences, buddies, invitations, and so forth in tables on a device, or instead use a web service and database in the cloud.

To facilitate a secure interaction when sending and receiving invitations and lists of preferences, we've decided to move all the database operations to the cloud. However, everything in this chapter is not only relevant to `ForgetMeNotDemo`; it will be of use to you if you decide to store data locally on a phone or computer.

Summary

In this chapter, we reviewed two ways of storing data. The simplest and most lightweight is to use the preferences facilities of .NET MAUI. This is great if all you need is to store primitives and short strings that are targeted at persisting a user's preferences for a program.

If you need to persist more substantial data, you'll need a database, and by far the most popular type for on-device storage is SQLite. We examined the CRUD functionality of SQLite and then pointed out the alternative of not storing everything on a device but, rather, storing in the cloud and gaining access through a program's API.

Quiz

1. What is the class that handles simple storage of user data in key/value pairs?
2. What two values do we pass to the Get method to retrieve the stored value?
3. Which NuGet packages do we need to work with SQLite in .NET MAUI?
4. What type of object do we use to create a table?

You try it

Add the remaining CRUD operations to the Preference table (for example, delete and get by ID).

9
Unit Testing

Until now, we've been focusing on creating the app, but there is danger in going too far without introducing unit testing. In this chapter, we will focus on writing comprehensive and meaningful unit tests using best practices.

> **Test-driven development (TDD)**
>
> Some developers believe that unit tests should come *before* the code (TDD), but that is beyond the scope of this book.

Unit testing is crucial to creating robust applications and knowing that your app works before you ship it. It is also a critical aspect of debugging, telling you right away if something you just changed or added broke some aspect of your app.

To facilitate unit tests, you'll want to use dependency injection so that you can mock up time-consuming services, such as APIs, databases, and so on. We'll spend time with mocks, injected into our test classes, to ensure that we are processing data as intended.

The specific topics in this chapter are as follows:

- Why create unit tests?
- Getting started creating unit tests
- Mocks
- Dependency injection
- NSubstitute

Technical requirements

To follow along with this chapter, you will need Visual Studio. You will also install two NuGet packages, as shown in the chapter itself. If you are going to enter the code as you go, you'll want to start with the source from the previous chapter: `https://github.com/PacktPublishing/.NET-MAUI-for-C-Sharp-Developers/tree/persistence`.

The source code for this chapter can be found here: `https://github.com/PacktPublishing/.NET-MAUI-for-C-Sharp-Developers/tree/UnitTests`.

Why create unit tests?

There are many types of tests you will want to run on a production app. These include unit tests (testing one small part of an app – typically, a method), integration tests (how well the parts of the program run together), UI tests (making sure that interacting with the UI acts as expected), and end-to-end tests (making sure the entire program works as expected).

Unit tests are a critical part of this process and are created for every method and every unit of logic. In fact, multiple tests are typically created for each unit, so that you can test the happy path, the sad path, and corner conditions.

The **happy path** is when the data is as expected. The **sad path** is when the data is predictably wrong (for example, the user does not enter a required field).

Corner conditions (also called **edge cases**) are those situations that are unlikely to happen but might (for example, the user enters `123` as the username).

A key benefit of unit tests is that they make your code less *brittle*. Without unit tests, it is easy to get into a situation where a change over here breaks code over there, and you don't know about the breakage until either you run the entire program or, worse, your customer finds it.

Key to all of this is that research has shown that it is easier and less expensive to fix a bug found during a unit test than it is to find bugs found later. For example, in the 1990s, Capers Jones analyzed data about bugs from more than 400 software projects and found that the cost of fixing a bug increased by a factor of 6 to 7 for every phase of development.

Furthermore, unit tests act as excellent documentation for your app, describing precisely what you expect to happen under a wide variety of situations. Unlike comments, which rust – that is, become out of sync with the code – unit tests can never depart from the code because they will break when your code changes in ways that make the expected outcome change.

Vote early and vote often

It is important to run all of your unit tests after every change you make to the code. You want to catch inadvertent and unwanted side effects as quickly as possible. However, for this to work, your unit tests must be *fast*. A suite of unit tests that take an appreciable amount of time to run will be used less often. The longer they take to run, the less frequently the programmer will run them.

Good unit tests are not only fast but also *isolated* from one another. That means that one unit test does not depend on the outcome or state of another – it should not matter what order they are run in.

You want to be able to look at the outcome of unit tests and immediately identify what went wrong so that you can fix it quickly. To accomplish this, your unit tests should do the following:

- Test exactly one thing at a time
- Be well named

If you test more than one thing in a unit test and that test fails, you won't know which of the things was the culprit. Well-named unit tests make it clear at a glance what they are testing and thus what went wrong.

This is an example of a bad unit test name: `DoesGetBuddiesWork`.

This is a good unit test name: `GettingBuddiesListDoesNotThrowAnException`.

If the test fails, a glance at the name of the *good unit test name* tells you exactly what went wrong.

> **Unit test names**
>
> Some programmers use very rigid naming schemes for unit tests. For example, some will create the name by the name of the method followed by the condition followed by the expected outcome. So, you might have a name like this: `GetBuddiesList_WhenEmpty_ShouldNotThrowAnException`.
>
> These can be useful, as glancing at the name of the test gives you a lot of information.

Remember, as the program grows, so too will your set of unit tests. When you have hundreds (or even thousands), you'll want to be able to zip through your tests so quickly that you don't mind running them after each meaningful change, and when one or more fail, you want to know what was tested without having to open up the test and look.

Creating unit tests

To get started, right-click on the solution and choose **Add New Project**. In the dialog box, use the dropdown to pick **UnitTest**. There are a number of unit test frameworks. The two most popular are the older **NUnit** and the newer **xUnit**. We'll choose **xUnit Test Project**, as shown in *Figure 9.1*:

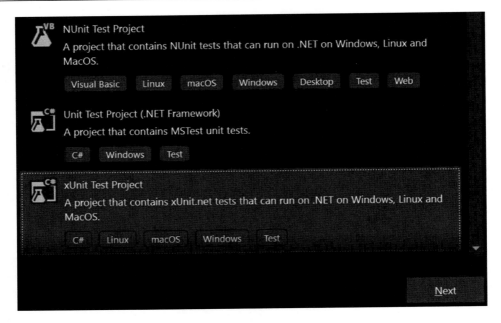

Figure 9.1 – Selecting the unit test type

1. Click **Next** and fill in the name and location of your new project. Typically, the name will be the name of the solution followed by `.Tests`, as shown in the following figure:

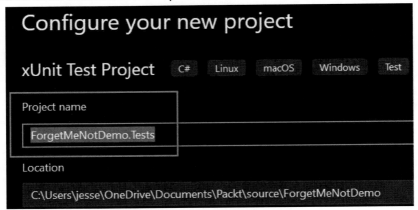

Figure 9.2 – Naming the test project

2. Click **Next** and select the .NET platform (this book will use .NET 7).

Visual Studio will create your project as well as the first unit test class and method. Since this is generic, delete that class and create one called `PreferencesTests`.

Setting the project reference

Before doing anything else, we need to make `ForgetMeNotDemo.Tests` aware of the `ForgetMeNotDemo` project. To do so, right-click on the test project and select **Add | ProjectReference**, and check the box next to **ForgetMeNotDemo**, as shown in *Figure 9.3*:

Reference Manager - ForgetMeNotDemoUnitTests

Figure 9.3 – Referencing ForgetMeNotDemo from the unit test project

With all that set up, we are ready to write our first unit test, designed only to ensure that the testing structure is in place and working.

> **Note**
>
> This will not build. Please refer to the *Tweaking the project file* section that appears later in the chapter.

Creating the first unit test

To make sure all is right with the world, open `UnitTest1` and add a test method that must pass:

```
namespace ForgetMeNotDemo.Tests
{
  public class UnitTest1
  {
    [Fact]
    public void MustBeTrue()
    {
      Assert.True(true);
    }
  }
}
```

xUnit tests come in two flavors:

- **Facts**: These are invariants – they always take the same data and should always pass

- **Theories**: These are a suite of tests that execute the same code but are given different input arguments

Let's explore the theories. The first test we created, `MustBeTrue`, simply asserts that the value true is `true`. This makes a good first test, as it will test that your unit testing is set up correctly.

To run this test, click on the **Test | Run All Tests** menu item – but be warned, *it won't work!*

In order to make this work, there is a bit of tweaking we have to do to the project file.

Tweaking the project file

The problem is that your .NET MAUI `.csproj` project file lists the following `TargetFrameworks`:

```
<TargetFrameworks>net7.0-android;net7.0-ios;net7.0-
    maccatalyst</TargetFrameworks>
```

However, the unit test project file looks like this:

```
<TargetFramework>7.0</TargetFramework>
```

To fix this discrepancy, exit Visual Studio and open your .NET MAUI project `.csproj` file using your favorite text editor (not Word or other programs that add special characters – I like to use Visual Studio Code, but whatever floats your boat). Modify `<TargetFramework>` to include .net7.0:

```
<TargetFrameworks>net7.0;net7.0-android;net7.0-ios;net7.0-
    maccatalyst</TargetFrameworks>
```

You're halfway there. The next issue is that we need to output the test as a DLL, but the output for the project is an EXE. The best way to fix this is to add a condition – only do the output as an EXE when the target framework is not 7.0:

```
<OutputType Condition="'$(TargetFramework)' !=
    'net7.0'">Exe</OutputType>
```

Reopen Visual Studio and open the solution. Your test should work now.

Running the test

First, rename `UnitTest1` to `PreferencesTests`. Next, go to the menu and select **Test | Test Explorer**. This will open (surprise!) **Test Explorer**. Click the green *Play* button, as shown in *Figure 9.4*:

Figure 9.4 – The Play button

Your project will build and Test Explorer will run your test, showing you results as shown in *Figure 9.5*:

Figure 9.5 – Test results

Reading down from the top, it shows that `ForgetMeNotDemo.Tests` has one test, and the green check indicates that all the tests in `ForgetMeNotDemo.Tests` have passed.

Inside `ForgetMeNotDemo.Tests` will be a list of all the test classes – in this case, just the one, `PreferencesTests`, and this too shows that there is one test and that it passed.

Finally, inside `PreferencesTests` will be a list of each individual test, and again, the green check indicates the test passed.

Congratulations, you've created your first test, run it, and seen it pass!

Now, let's settle down to writing some tests for `ForgetMeNotDemo`.

ForgetMeNotDemo unit tests

To get started, we examine one ViewModel at a time, paying attention to the methods. We do this because what we want to test is the business logic, and if you've done it right, most of your business logic will be in a `ViewModel` class.

For example, turning our attention to `PreferencesViewModel`, we see the `Init()` method. The job of `Init` is to populate the `PreferenceList` collection. For now, we'll ignore how it does this and just write a test to ensure that it does.

Implementing the triple-A pattern

Before we start, create an interface for `PreferenceService`, as described earlier in the book (open `PreferenceService`, right-click on the class name, and choose **Extract Interface**).

A classic design pattern for unit tests is the **Arrange, Act, Assert** (**AAA**) pattern. That is, you set up your test (Arrange), then you call a method or two (Act), and then check to make sure you have the expected results (Assert). Let's see this in action (note, this test has two flaws that will be discussed):

```
[Fact]
public async void AfterCallingInitPreferencesIsNotEmpty()
{
  // Arrange
  IPreferenceService service = new PreferenceService();
  preferencesViewModel = new PreferencesViewModel();


  // Act
  await preferencesViewModel.Init();


  // Assert
  Assert.NotEmpty(preferencesViewModel.PreferenceList);
}
```

Here, we set up `IPreferenceService`, which we'll need to create `PreferencesViewModel`, and then we create an instance of that `ViewModel`.

With that in place, we can call the `Init()` method.

Now, we will test the results using Assert. Assert has many methods that you can use to test the success of your test. These include, but are not limited to, the following:

- `Assert.True`
- `Assert.False`
- `Assert.Equal<T>(T expected, T actual)`
- `Assert.InRange<T>(T actual, T low, T high)`
- `Assert.Null`
- `Assert.NotNull`
- `Assert.IsType<T>(object obj)`
- `Assert.Empty(IenumerableCollection)`
- `Assert.Contains<T>(T expected, Ienumerable<t> collection)`

There are many more too. The definitive list can be found at the xUnit repository: `https://github.com/xunit/assert.xunit/blob/main/Assert.cs`. The various Asserts are arranged as classes, each of which has a variety of `Assert` methods. A partial list is shown in *Figure 9.6*:

Figure 9.6 – A partial list of Assert classes

In our case, we are asserting that, after running `Init`, `PreferenceList` is not empty. Open **Test Explorer** and click on the **Run All Tests In View** button, as shown here:

Figure 9.7 – Run All Tests In View button

The tests run, and Test Explorer gives us the results, as shown in the following figure:

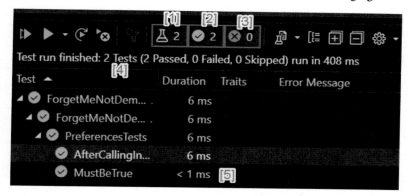

Figure 9.8 – Test Explorer results

Let us see what each numbered option in the figure means:

[1] The number of tests

[2] The number of tests that passed

[3] The number of tests that failed

[4] A summary and statement on how long the test took

[5] Each passed test in the context of where the text is located. A green check means that it passed, and a red x indicates that it failed. Notice that the time for each test is listed. Also note that the tests took at most 6 milliseconds, but the entire test suite took 408 ms. The difference is the overhead of beginning the test procedure. This will soon be swamped by the time for all the tests.

What's wrong with this test?

I mentioned previously that this test has two significant flaws. The first is that the call to Init may not populate PreferenceList because the service may return zero records. We'll need to adjust for that by asserting instead that PreferenceList is not null.

The second, more important, problem is that the test depends on running PreferenceService. If we examine the code for PreferenceService, we see that the call to GetPreferences has a significant problem:

```
public async Task<List<Preference>> GetPreferences()
{
    return await GetPreferencesMock();
}
```

Right now, while developing the app, we are calling to GetPreferencesMock, which is just a method in PreferenceService. But that is not how we'll finish the app. In *Chapter 11*, we'll convert this to make an API call. API calls can take an unpredictably long time, and potentially, can grind our test to a halt.

To solve this, we need a mock PreferenceService that both returns quickly and returns a predictable collection (or an empty collection if we want to test that eventuality).

Mocks

Often, when testing, you need to interact with a method that takes an indeterminate amount of time, such as retrieving data from a database or, worse, retrieving data from an API (that is, over the internet rather than locally from your device).

Calling this kind of method can bring your unit test to a screeching halt, making it almost unusable. To avoid this, we create fake representations of the database or the API using an object called a **mock**.

Mocks offer two advantages: they respond instantly and, perhaps as importantly, they respond predictably. Once written, they give the same input and mock will always provide the same output.

In order to use mocks, we'll need to implement dependency injection for some of our classes, so let's start there.

Dependency injection

Until now, anytime we needed an object inside a class, we passed in the object or we created it in the body of the class. This creates a **dependency** (the receiving method is dependent on the object passed in or created.) This approach creates **tight coupling** – which just means that both classes are coupled together and changing one risks having to change the other. For example, in `PreferencesViewModel`, we need a `PreferenceService` object. The approach we've taken so far is to *new one up* in the constructor:

```
private readonly PreferenceService service;

public PreferencesViewModel()
{
  service = new();
}
```

Dependency injection decouples the classes and allows for more powerful unit testing, as we'll see when we continue the discussion of mocks. Rather than *newing-up* a `PreferenceService`, we want to pass in an interface and have .NET MAUI create it for us (that is, no calling function will add the interface to the constructor call – it will be done automatically).

> **Not just for testing**
>
> Dependency injection can be used throughout your project, not only for unit tests. In fact, when combined with an **Inversion of Control** (**IoC**) container, dependency injection creates a powerful pattern for decoupling objects throughout the app. More on IoC containers later.

Creating an interface

To do this, we first need to create an `IPreferenceService` interface.

> **Resharper**
>
> Everything I'm about to show uses **Resharper**, an essential tool for serious .NET MAUI programmers, but it is not free. You can certainly do all this by hand; it is just that Resharper makes it much easier. Since I highly recommend buying Resharper, I'll show you how to do the following with that tool. (Please note, as a Microsoft MVP, I get my copy of Resharper for free.)

First, go to **Solution Explorer**, open **PreferenceService**, and follow these steps:

1. Right-click on the class name and choose **Refactor This**. A context menu will appear, as shown in the following figure:

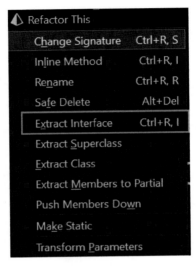

Figure 9.9 – Refactor context menu

2. Select **Extract Interface**, and a dialog box will appear as shown here:

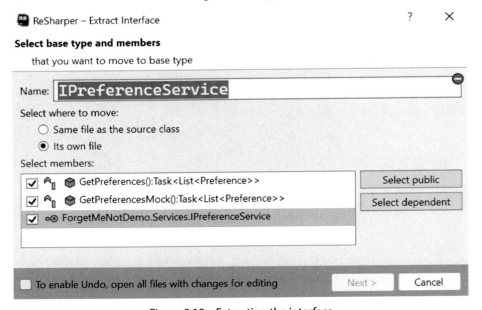

Figure 9.10 – Extracting the interface

3. Be sure to check all the public methods and choose the **Its own file** radio button for where to move the interface.

Hey, presto! You'll have an interface file in the same directory (`Services`), as shown in *Figure 9.11*:

Figure 9.11 – New interface file in the Services folder

Open your new file and you'll see a typical C# interface:

```
public interface IPreferenceService
{
  public Task<List<Preference>> GetPreferences();
  public Task<List<Preference>> GetPreferencesMock();
}
```

Now, check the original `PreferenceService`. Resharper was nice enough to designate that `PreferenceService` implements `IPreferenceService`:

```
public class PreferenceService : IPreferenceService
```

Please make `PreferenceService.GetPreferencesMock` public.

With an interface, we can use constructor injection – that is, we can define that we're going to pass an instance of the interface into the constructor, and then pass in anything that implements that interface.

Modifying the class constructor

Let's go back to `PreferencesViewModel`. Since we know we're going to use dependency injection to send `PreferenceService` into `ViewModel`, we can modify the declaration of `PreferenceService` and the constructor:

```
Private readonly IPreferenceService service;    [1]

public PreferencesViewModel(IPreferenceService service) [2]
{
  this.service = service; [3]
}
```

[1] We change the local service member to an interface.

[2] We pass IPreferenceService into the constructor.

[3] We assign the member to the passed-in parameter.

But who calls PreferencesViewModel with the IPreference service, and where does that method get it?

The answer is that the IoC container is responsible for all of this.

The .NET MAUI IoC container

.NET MAUI has a built-in IoC container that we use by registering the interfaces we want to be managed. You do this in the CreateMauiApp method in MauiProgram.cs:

```
public static MauiApp CreateMauiApp()
{
    var builder = MauiApp.CreateBuilder(); [1]
    builder
    .UseMauiApp<App>()
    .UseMauiCommunityToolkit()
    .UseMauiCommunityToolkitMarkup()
    .ConfigureFonts(fonts =>
    {
      fonts.AddFont("OpenSans-Regular.ttf",
        "OpenSansRegular");
      fonts.AddFont("OpenSans-Semibold.ttf",
        "OpenSansSemibold");
    })
    .UseMauiMaps();

if DEBUG
    builder.Logging.AddDebug();
endif

    return builder.Build();
}
```

As seen in [1], the first thing we do is instantiate a MauiAppBuilder object. We then tack a number of other configuration requirements onto the Builder.

We'll use that to register all the interfaces to all our services. In fact, we'll also register our views and ViewModels so that we can pass them into methods using dependency injection.

Registering your interfaces, services, and ViewModels

.NET MAUI provides an IoC container. By registering our interfaces, services, and so on, .NET MAUI will supply what we need when we need it, without our having to *new-up* instances. Beyond that, the IoC container will also fix up all the dependencies.

To register the `IPreferences` interface, we add a call to `Builder.Services.AddTransient`, passing in the interface and the class that implements that interface:

```
builder.Services.AddTransient<IPreferenceService,
    PreferenceService>();
```

`Builder.Services` offers two ways to register your interface:

- `AddTransient`
- `AddSingleton`

You'll use `AddTransient` when you may or may not instantiate the object (we may never look at the user's preferences, and thus may never need the service). You use `AddSingleton` when you know you'll want the object and there is no point in creating more than one.

While we're here, let's register all the ViewModels. We don't need interfaces for them, as we won't be passing them anywhere via dependency injection:

```
builder.Services.AddTransient<AboutViewModel>();
builder.Services.AddTransient<BuddiesViewModel>();
builder.Services.AddTransient<BuddyDetailsViewModel>();
builder.Services.AddTransient<PreferencesViewModel>();
builder.Services.AddTransient<LoginViewModel>();
```

Putting it together, this is what `CreateMauiApp` looks like now:

```
public static MauiApp CreateMauiApp()
{
    var builder = MauiApp.CreateBuilder();
  builder
    .UseMauiApp<App>()
    .UseMauiCommunityToolkit()
    .UseMauiCommunityToolkitMarkup()
```

```
      .ConfigureFonts(fonts =>
      {
        fonts.AddFont("OpenSans-Regular.ttf",
          "OpenSansRegular");
        fonts.AddFont("OpenSans-Semibold.ttf",
          "OpenSansSemibold");
      })
      .UseMauiMaps();

  if DEBUG
      builder.Logging.AddDebug();
  endif

    builder.Services.AddTransient<IPreferenceService,
      PreferenceService>();

    builder.Services.AddTransient<AboutViewModel>();
    builder.Services.AddTransient<BuddyDetailsViewModel>();
    builder.Services.AddTransient<PreferencesViewModel>();
    builder.Services.AddTransient<LoginViewModel>();

    return builder.Build();
  }
```

Notice that all the registration happens before we return the result of calling `Build` on the `Builder` object.

We will be using dependency injection to inject mock objects where objects that would otherwise take an unpredictable amount of time would normally be used. That is, rather than waiting for a database or API call, we can inject a mock database or a mock service and get back a response instantly and predictably.

Our first decision is which mocking library to use.

Using the NSubstitute package

There are a number of different mocking libraries available to you, some free and some commercial. For this book, we'll use **NSubstitute**, an open source and free option available as a NuGet package.

To get started, follow these steps:

1. Right-click on your solution and choose **ManageNugetPackagesForSolution**.

2. Go to the **Browse** tab and enter NSubstitute.

   The first package you want is **NSubstitute** by Anthony Egerton et al., as shown here:

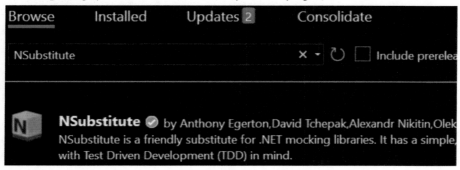

Figure 9.12 – NSubstitute NuGet package

3. On the right, click on the project you want this added to (ForgetMeNotDemo.Tests) and click on **Install**, as shown in *Figure 9.13*:

Figure 9.13 – Installing NSubstitute

4. Once that installs, install **NSubstitute.Analyzers.CSharp**, as shown in the following figure:

Figure 9.14 – Selecting NSubstitute.Analyzers.CSharp

While not strictly required, this second library will detect potential mistakes in your use of NSubstitute. Install it into the test project as you did previously.

Adding NSubstitute to your test fixture

To add NSubstitute to your test fixture, add `using NSubstitute;` to the top of the C# file.

We can now create a substitute for `PreferenceService`.

Mocks depend on constructor dependency injection

Turn to the constructor in `PreferencesViewModel` and notice that the service is injected as an interface:

```
public PreferencesViewModel(IPreferenceService service)

  {

    this.service = service;

  }
```

This is critical. Mocks only work with constructor injection.

Back in our unit test, let's declare a mock for the service:

```
[Fact]
public async void AfterCallingInitPreferencesIsNotEmpty()
{
  // Arrange
  var service = Substitute.For<IPreferenceService>();    [1]
  var = new PreferencesViewModel(service); [2]


  // Act
  await preferencesViewModel.Init();


  // Assert
  Assert.NotEmpty(preferencesViewModel.PreferenceList);
}
```

[1] Declare the mock for `IpreferenceService`.

[2] Pass that mock into the constructor for `PreferencesViewModel`.

Run the test. It fails with the error that the collection cannot be null. Why?

The original service was returning a list of `Preference` objects, but our new mock is not. We need to teach the mock to return a predictable set of `Preference` objects.

Here is the top of the `Arrange` method, in which we create a couple of `Preference` objects and then add them to a list:

```
public async void AfterCallingInitPreferencesIsNotEmpty()
{
  // Arrange

  Preference pref1 = new()
  {
    Id = 1,
    PreferencePrompt = "Shirt Size",
    PreferenceValue = "Large"
  };

  Preference pref2 = new()
  {
    PreferencePrompt = "Favorite Music Genre",
    PreferenceValue = "Jazz"
  };

  List<Preference> prefs = new()
  {
    pref1,
    pref2
  };
```

We can now create our substitute:

```
var serviceMock = Substitute.For<IPreferenceService>(); [1]
  serviceMock.GetPreferences() [2]
  .Returns(prefs); [3]
```

[1] Create the mock.

[2] Tell the mock which method it will be mocking.

[3] Tell the mock what to return when that method is invoked.

We use the mock in calling the `PreferencesViewModel` constructor, which you will remember takes `IpreferenceService`:

```
preferencesViewModel = new PreferencesViewModel
    (serviceMock);
```

In the `Act` portion of the test, we'll call `Init` on that `PreferencesViewModel` object and then assert that the list is not empty. This will work this time because the service it relies on can now be predicted to return a list of two preferences.

Testing corner cases

What happens if `PreferenceService` returns no records? Will that cause `ViewModel` to blow up? We can test that:

```
[Fact]
public async void AfterCallingInitPreferencesIsEmptyButNo
    Exception()
{
    // Arrange
    List<Preference> preferences = new(); [1]

    var serviceMock = Substitute.For<IPreferenceService>();
    serviceMock.GetPreferences()
        .Returns(preferences); [2]


    preferencesViewModel = new PreferencesViewModel
        (serviceMock);

    // Act
    var exception = await Record.ExceptionAsync (async ()
        => await preferencesViewModel.Init()); [3]

    // Assert
    Assert.Null(exception); [4]
}
```

[1] Set up `List<Preference>` to be empty.

[2] Have the service return the empty preferences list.

[3] Use `Record.ExceptionAsync` and pass in the call to `Init`. This will return the exception or null if none was thrown.

[4] Assert that there was no exception thrown.

A complete description of all the uses of NSubstitute is available at `https://nsubstitute.github.io/help.html`.

Summary

In this chapter, we reviewed the critical importance of writing unit tests and comprehensively testing your program. In a nutshell, unit tests allow you to code with confidence, knowing that if you make a change and it breaks something seemingly unrelated, you'll find out about it immediately.

We saw that, at times, your unit test must interact with slower external systems (APIs, databases, and more) and that you can keep your subsecond response time by using mocks; the mocking library we chose is `NSubstitute`, though there are other free mocking systems as well (a very popular one is **Moq**).

In order to facilitate using mocks, we looked at dependency injection and briefly reviewed the role of IoC containers. In the next chapter, *Consuming a Rest Service*, we will look at getting our data from a cloud-based (Azure) service, rather than mocking the data.

Quiz

1.   Why is it important to write unit tests?
2.   Where is most of the code you will test?
3.   Why do you use mocks?
4.   Why is dependency injection important for mocks?

You try it

Identify a method in the ViewModel or service that interacts with the API or database, and write a unit test that uses a mock.

Part 3 – Advanced Topics

In this final part, we will dive into ninja-level topics, including how to interact with a REST-based service (in our case, Azure) and how to modify the appearance of our app based on the runtime data.

This part has the following chapters:

10
Consuming REST Services

Up until now, when we needed data, we faked it by using hardcoded objects. In a real-world program, however, you will get most of your data from local databases (as discussed in *Chapter 8*), or you will interact with a service in the cloud through an API. You can interact using one of several architectures, of which the most popular for .NET MAUI is, arguably, **Representational State Transfer** (**REST**).

REST is a pattern that describes how classes interact across the internet. The key to REST is that it is stateless – that is, a sustained connection between the client and the API is not needed.

The Forget Me Not architecture is designed to use a REST service and database, which will manage membership, authentication, and persistence of user data. In this chapter, we will look at the following:

- Using REST services
- The Forget Me Not API architecture
- API domain objects
- **Data Transfer Objects** (**DTOs**)
- The API Client class
- Using the API

Technical requirements

To follow along with this chapter, you will need Visual Studio. If you are going to enter the code as you follow along, you'll want the branch for the previous chapter.

The source code for the finished project for this chapter can be found at `https://github.com/PacktPublishing/.NET-MAUI-for-C-Sharp-Developers/tree/REST`.

Using REST Services

Until now, all the work we've been doing has been local to a device (a phone, Windows, or Mac). The design of Forget Me Not entails the use of a service in the cloud that will manage all our data – invitations to a program, registration, authentication, data persistence, and so on.

A client interacts with a server through a **REST API** (also called a RESTful API).

An **Application Program Interface** (**API**) is a set of definitions and protocols to interact with an application. In our case, the API we care about is the cloud-based `ForgetMeNot.API`.

Knowing more about REST

For our purposes, that is really all you need to know about REST, but if you are curious, you can find out more at `https://en.wikipedia.org/wiki/Representational_state_transfer`.

The Forget Me Not API architecture

When we looked at getting a user's preferences in *Chapter 8*, we used the Preference Service. That service, until now, used a method to return hardcoded values. That, of course, was a temporary expedient so that we could focus on one thing at a time. We are ready now to interact with the online API.

Where's the service?

I have created an online web service on Azure at `https://forgetmenota-pi20230113114628.azurewebsites.net/`.

It is my goal to keep this up and running so that you can implement the client and get meaningful results, but given that there may be maintenance costs, by the time you read this, the service may no longer be in place. If that is true, you can still get 95% of what you need by reading the API code and using hardcoded data, as we've been doing up until now.

Also, note that just going to the URL won't get you anywhere. It is when we combine that base URL with the specific task-based additions that the magic happens. You can test whether the API is still available by creating an account or signing into one. If that works, then the rest of the API should work as well.

To facilitate our REST interactions with the API, we will use the extremely popular open source `RestSharp` library (`https://restsharp.dev/`). It will do all the heavy lifting for us. (We'll be using the `class` library template.)

Creating the projects

To get started, we'll need three new projects. Right-click on **Solution** and choose **Add New Project**. The three projects are named:

- `ForgetMeNot.API.Domain` (API domain objects)
- `ForgetMeNot.API.Dto` (DTOs)
- `ForgetMeNot.ApiClient` (a wrapper for the API)

`Api.Doman` and `API.Dto` are both class libraries. `APIClient` is a `webapi`.

We'll look at each of these in turn, filling in all the details.

Because we'll be using the API database, we can remove the local SQLite database. To do so, comment out or remove the `Constants` file and the entire `ForgetMeNotDemoDatabase.cs` file.

Fleshing out the models

Before we create classes that correspond to the items in our model classes, we need to flesh them out.

Let's start with the `Preference` class in the `Model` directory. We had added an `Id` property for SQLite; we won't need that anymore, so we can remove it. Remove it from `PreferencesTests.AfterCallingInitPreferencesIsNotEmpty()` as well.

The design spec says that a user can invite a friend to be a buddy. We'll need to add a model to describe the invitation:

```
using CommunityToolkit.Mvvm.ComponentModel;


namespace ForgetMeNotDemo.Model;


[ObservableObject]
public partial class Invitation
{

  [ObservableProperty] private string buddyCode;
  [ObservableProperty] private int buddyId;
}
```

Similarly, we need to keep track of *occasions*, such as birthdays and anniversaries, so that we remember to use Forget Me Not to buy a present:

```
[ObservableObject]
public partial class Occasion
{
   [ObservableProperty] private string name;
   [ObservableProperty] private DateTime date;
   [ObservableProperty] private int numDaysToNotify;
}
```

We'll need a couple more Model classes, such as User and its derived class, Buddy. The owner of the app is a user, as are all their buddies. Here is the User Model class:

```
[ObservableObject]
public partial class User
{
   [ObservableProperty] private string name;

   [ObservableProperty] private string id;      [1]

   [ObservableProperty] private List<Buddy> buddies;  [2]

   [ObservableProperty] private List<Invitation>
     invitations; [3]

   [ObservableProperty] private List<Preference>
     preferences; [4]
```

[1] We've migrated the ID up here to the base class. We won't need it for the (now non-existent) local database, but we will need the ID on the server. It is a string because the server will create a **Globally Unique ID (GUID).**

[2] Each user can have any number of Buddies.

[3] Each user can send out any number of invitations.

[4] Each user will have a list of Preference objects.

> **Commented-out code**
>
> Note that the `invitations` property is commented out in the code present in the GitHub repository. Please uncomment it.

The Buddy class builds on this:

```
public partial class Buddy : User
{
    [ObservableProperty] private string emailAddress;
    [ObservableProperty] private string? phoneNumber;
    [ObservableProperty] private string? mailingAddressLine1;
    [ObservableProperty] private string? mailingAddressLine2;
    [ObservableProperty] private string? website;
    [ObservableProperty] private string? twitter;
    [ObservableProperty] private string? facebook;
    [ObservableProperty] private string? instagram;
    [ObservableProperty] private string? linkedIn;
    [ObservableProperty] private string? venmoName;

    [ObservableProperty] private InvitationStatus status;

    [ObservableProperty] private List<OccasionModel>
      occasions;

    [ObservableProperty] private DateTime buddySince;
}
```

> **Commented-out code**
>
> For now, do not uncomment `InvitationStatus` or `OccasionModel`.

We store a lot of information about each buddy, including how long they've been our buddy, shared occasions, and the status of the invitation we sent to the Buddy class.

Examining the API domain objects

The API domain objects are a superset of the `client model` classes. This is because there is data that the API will need that will not be visible on the client side. Right-click on **ForgetMeNot.API. Domain** and create the following classes:

- `InvitationStatus`
- `Invite`
- `Occasion`
- `Related`
- `Roles`
- `User`
- `UserPreference`

Let's walk through them, starting with `User` (note that this uses `UserPreference`, defined in the following code, so do not build until you have both classes):

```
public class User
{
    public Guid Id { get; set; }
    public string FullName { get; set; }
    public string Email { get; set; }
    public string HashedPassword { get; set; }
    public bool IsEmailConfirmed { get; set; }
    public string Role { get; set; }
    public List<UserPreference> Preferences { get; set; }
}
```

As you can see, on the server, each `User` instance has a unique ID. Most of the other properties are the same as on the client, although they may not have the same identifier (for example, `FullName` rather than Name). This is not a problem, as we'll do the mapping when we get the objects from the server.

There are a few new fields, however – for example, `IsEmailConfirmed`, `HashedPassword`, and `Role`. These are used by the server for authentication.

Let's create the `Roles` file. It is a static class with the two roles we'll support:

```
public static class Roles
{
    public static string Admin = "admin";
```

```
    public static string User = "user";
}
```

Next, we'll turn our attention to the `UserPreference` class. This corresponds to the `Preference` class in our client's `Model` folder:

```
public class UserPreference
{
    public string PreferencePrompt { get; set; }
    public string PreferenceValue { get; set; }
}
```

Note that the API is, in some ways, independent of the client. We're calling the class by a different name, and we're not using the code generators.

Next, we need classes to represent `Invitation` and `Occasion`. Let's start with `Invitation`:

```
public class Invite
{
    public Invite()
    {
        Id = Guid.NewGuid();
    }

    public Guid Id { get; set; }
    public User CreatedByUser { get; set; }
    public User? AcceptedByUser { get; set; }
    public InvitationStatus Status { get; set; }
    public DateTime CreationDate { get; set; }
    public DateTime? EndDate { get; set; }
    public string InvitedUserName { get; set; }
    public string InvitedUserCustomMessage { get; set; }
}
```

This class has a property of the `InvitationStatus` type. Create a file for that as well. This is just an enumeration:

```
public enum InvitationStatus
{
    Waiting,
```

```
        Expired,
        Accepted,
        Rejected
    }
```

Here's the Occasion class:

```
public class Occasion
{
    public Occasion()
    {
        Id = Guid.NewGuid();
    }
    public Guid Id { get; set; }
    public User? ForUser { get; set; }
    public string? OccasionName { get; set; }
    public DateTime Date { get; set; }
    public int NumDaysToNotify { get; set; }
}
```

The purpose of NumDaysToNotify is to allow a user to designate how many days in advance of an occasion they want to be notified (that functionality is left as an exercise for you!).

Finally, we add a class whose job is to tie a user to all their Occasions and buddies. Note that we use User for Buddy, as the base class has all the information we need:

```
public class Related
{
    public Related()
    {
        Occasions = new List<Occasion>();
        Users = new List<User>();
    }

    public Guid Id { get; set; }
    public string RelatedDescription { get; set; }

    public List<User> Users { get; set; }
    public List<Occasion> Occasions { get; set; }
```

```
      public DateTime Since { get; set; }
}
```

That's it for that project. There are no methods; it really is just a set of server-based model objects.

Once we have the models, we need to determine how to transfer this data to and from the server. For that, we need DTOs.

Reviewing DTOs

The `ForgetMeNot.Api.Dto` project will, as you might have guessed, hold DTOs. These will correspond to the model objects but are designed to be passed back and forth between the server and the client.

> **Project reference**
>
> You will need to add a project reference from `ForgetMeNot.Api.Dto` to `ForgetMeNot.Api.Domain`.

Let's start with `BuddyDto.cs`:

```
using ForgetMeNot.Api.Domain;

namespace ForgetMeNot.Api.Dto
{
    public class BuddyDto
    {
        public BuddyDto()
        {
        }

        public BuddyDto(User user)
        {
            UserId = user.Id;
            FullName = user.FullName;
            Email = user.Email;

            Preferences = new List<UserPreference>();
            if (user.Preferences?.Any(p =>
                p.PreferenceValue != null) ?? false)
```

```
            {
                Preferences = user.Preferences.Where(p =>
                    p.PreferenceValue != null).ToList();
            }

            Occasions = new List<OccasionDto>();
        }

        public Guid UserId { get; set; }
        public string FullName { get; set; }
        public string Email { get; set; }
        public List<UserPreference> Preferences { get; set; }
        public List<OccasionDto> Occasions { get; set; }
    }
}
```

Note that the constructor for Buddy takes User. As noted earlier, the Buddy class derives from User, and by passing User into the constructor, we can set Buddy's User properties.

Note that we are also using a list of OccasionDto objects. These are in the ForgetMeNot.Api. Dto project.

Other DTO files

The other key files in ForgetMeNot.Api.Dto are not tied to model classes but, rather, are data that is exchanged between client and server to facilitate managing the account – for example, AccountCreateRequest:

```
public class AccountCreateRequest
{
    public string FullName { get; set; }
    public string Email { get; set; }
    public string PlainPassword { get; set; }
}
```

This is all that needs to be sent to the server when creating an account. There is a DTO to request an update to a user record that just contains `Id`, `FullName`, and `Email`. One important DTO is `UserResponse`, which contains information that corresponds to the `User` Domain object:

```
public class UserResponse
{
  public Guid Id { get; set; }
  public string FullName { get; set; }
  public string Email { get; set; }
  public bool IsEmailConfirmed { get; set; }
  public string Role { get; set; }

  public List<UserPreference> Preferences { get; set; }

  public UserResponse()
  {

  }

  public UserResponse(User user)
  {
    Id = user.Id;
    FullName = user.FullName;
    Email = user.Email;
    Role = user.Role;
    IsEmailConfirmed = user.IsEmailConfirmed;
    Preferences = user.Preferences;
  }
}
```

You pass in a `User` object and `UserResponse` turns it into a DTO.

Similarly, you can pass a `User` object into `ProfileResponse` and get back a `ProfileResponse` DTO:

```
public class ProfileResponse
{
  public Guid Id { get; set; }
  public string FullName { get; set; }
```

```
    public string Email { get; set; }
    public bool IsEmailConfirmed { get; set; }
    public string Role { get; set; }
    public List<UserPreference> Preferences { get; set; }

    public ProfileResponse(User user)
    {
      Id = user.Id;
      FullName = user.FullName;
      Email = user.Email;
      Role = user.Role;
      IsEmailConfirmed = user.IsEmailConfirmed;
      Preferences = user.Preferences;
    }
  }
}
```

The final piece in the puzzle is to wrap the API in a client-side class to facilitate interactions with data in the cloud.

Understanding ForgetMeNot.APIClient

The third API project, ForgetMeNot.APIClient, has only one class in it – Client.cs. This is the wrapper of the REST service that the client (ForgetMeNotDemo) will interact with.

We start with four member variables:

```
public class Client
{
    RestClient client;  [1]

    string baseUrl;    [2]
    string username;   [3]
    string password;
```

[1] As noted earlier, RestClient is the library we are using to manage the REST interactions (obtained through NuGet, as discussed earlier).

[2] baseURL is the prefix for all the API calls and was created when we moved the API to Azure. As noted earlier, it is available at https://forgetmenotapi20230113114628. azurewebsites.net/.

[3] username and password are used by the client to access the user's record.

The constructor to Client takes baseUrl, assigns it to the field, and then calls SetClient():

```
public Client(string baseUrl)
{
    this.baseUrl = baseUrl;
    SetClient();
}

void SetClient()
{
    var options = new RestClientOptions(baseUrl)    [1]
    {
        ThrowOnAnyError = false,
        MaxTimeout = 10000
    };

    client = new RestClient(options);  [2]
}
```

[1] The options we want for this REST client create a robust interface; we won't throw an exception on any error and we won't time out for 10 seconds.

[2] With the options set, we can create a new RestClient, which is defined in RestSharp.

The rest of the file is divided into sections for important behavior by the client, beginning with the code needed to authenticate the user.

Authentication

We set a IsAuthenticated property, which is set to whether or not client.Authenticator is null.

We then have a Login method that takes a LoginRequest object, sets username and password, and calls Authenticate:

```
public async Task Login(LoginRequest request)
{
    username = request.Username;
```

```
        password = request.Password;

        await Authenticate();
}
```

> **Project reference**
> You will need a reference to the DTO project.

LoginRequest is defined in the DTO project and simply has two string properties, Username and Password (refer to the following code block).

The Authenticate method uses RestSharp's OAuth authentication – that is, again, the heavy lifting is done by RestSharp:

```
async Task Authenticate()
{
    var request = new RestRequest("auth/gettoken");
    request.AddBody(new { username, password });

    var accessToken = await client.PostAsync<string>
        (request);

    client.Authenticator = new OAuth2Authorization
        RequestHeaderAuthenticator(accessToken, "Bearer");
}
```

Fortunately, you don't need to understand how to make this work; you just pass in the username and password and RestSharp takes care of the rest of it for you.

> **Client versus client**
> Remember that even though you are in the Client class, the client field is the RestSharp object.

We have a helper method to get the current API version:

```
public Task<string?> Version()
{
```

```
    var request = new RestRequest("util/version");

    return client.GetAsync<string?>(request);
}
```

And that takes us to the profile section of the file, where we can get and update the `profile` object.

Profile

There are two methods needed for the profile. The first gets the profile:

```
public Task<ProfileResponse?> GetProfile()
{
    var request = new RestRequest("profile/me");

    return client.GetAsync<ProfileResponse?>(request);
}
```

This uses the `ProfileResponse` DTO we examined earlier. The second method in this section is used to update the profile:

```
public Task UpdateProfile(ProfileUpdateRequest
    profileUpdateRequest)
{
    var request = new RestRequest("profile/me");

    request.AddBody(profileUpdateRequest);

    return client.PutAsync(request);
}
```

This code uses the `ProfileUpdateRequest` object defined in `ForgetMeNot.Api.Dto`.

Again, all the interesting work here is being done by `RestSharp`. As you can see, the client is really just a wrapper around the `RestSharp` methods.

Let's reinforce this by looking at a couple more methods that are used to manage the `Buddy` object.

The Buddy region

This region consists of the methods we need to interact with buddies, `GetBuddy` and `CreateInvitation`. GetBuddy returns a list of `BuddyDto` objects:

```
public Task<List<BuddyDto>?> GetBuddy()
{
    var request = new RestRequest("buddy");
    return client.GetAsync<List<BuddyDto>?>(request);
}
```

`CreateInvitation` returns Guid, which is the `Id` attribute of the resulting `Invitation` object:

```
public Task<Guid?> CreateInvitation(InviteCreateRequest
  inviteCreateRequest)
{
    var request = new RestRequest("buddy/invite");
    request.AddBody(inviteCreateRequest);
    return client.PostAsync<Guid?>(request);
}
```

This code uses `InviteCreateRequest`, which is defined in `ForgetMeNot.Api.Dto`.

Finally, we have a method to get all the users – that is, all this user's buddies:

```
public Task<List<UserResponse>?> GetUserList()
{
    var request = new RestRequest("user");

    return client.GetAsync<List<UserResponse>?>(request);
}
```

What we get back is a list of `UserResponse` DTO objects that we saw earlier.

Now that we've examined all the projects provided by the server, we are ready to have `ForgetMeNotDemo` interact with the API to get, store, and retrieve data.

Using the API

With the `Client` class and its supporting `DTO` and `API` domain classes in place, we're ready to interact with the API to create accounts and log in, as well as store and retrieve our preferences.

Creating the account

The first thing a new user will do is create an account. To make this work, we need to bring the user to the **Login** page when the app starts. Here, the user can log in, or if they don't have an account, they can click on **Create Account**, which will take them to CreateAccount.xaml, where they can fill in their name, email, and password. To implement this, we have to make some substantial changes to the **Login** and **Create Account** pages.

Let's begin by pointing the application to start with login. Modify the App.xaml.cs App method to look like this:

```
public App(LoginViewModel loginViewModel)  [1]
{
  InitializeComponent();
  MainPage = new LoginPage(loginViewModel);  [2]
}
```

[1] Have the IoC container pass in an instance of LoginViewModel.

[2] Set MainPage (the entry point to the program) to LoginPage.

The job of the **Login** page will now be to either allow the user to log in or take them to the **Create Account** page.

Be sure to add routing for CreateAccount in AppShell.xaml.cs:

```
Routing.RegisterRoute("createaccount",
  typeof(CreateAccountPage));
```

Next, let's modify the **Login** page.

Modifying the Login page

Now that we're going to turn management of authentication over to the server, we need a different **Login** page. Completely empty out LoginPage.xaml.cs and replace it with this simple version:

```
using CommunityToolkit.Maui.Core.Views;
using ForgetMeNotDemo.ViewModel;

namespace ForgetMeNotDemo.View;

public partial class LoginPage : ContentPage
{
```

```
  public LoginPage(LoginViewModel viewModel)
  {
    BindingContext = viewModel;
    InitializeComponent();
  }
}
```

LoginViewModel is passed in from App, as shown in the preceding code.

Now, let's modify LoginPage to focus on either logging a user in or redirecting them to create a new account.

Updating LoginPage

We're going to make some significant changes to LoginPage. To avoid confusion, delete all you have there and replace it with this:

```
<?xml version="1.0" encoding="utf-8" ?>
<ContentPage
    x:Class="ForgetMeNot.View.LoginPage"
    xmlns="http://schemas.microsoft.com/dotnet/2021/maui"
    xmlns:x="http://schemas.microsoft.com/winfx/2009/xaml"
    xmlns:iOsSpecific="clr-namespace:Microsoft.Maui
      .Controls.PlatformConfiguration.iOSSpecific;
        assembly=Microsoft.Maui.Controls"
    Title="Login"
    iOsSpecific:Page.UseSafeArea="True"
    Shell.NavBarIsVisible="False"
    Shell.PresentationMode="ModalAnimated">
    <ContentPage.Resources>
        <ResourceDictionary>
            <Style x:Key="Prompt" TargetType="Label">    [1]
                <Setter Property="TextColor" Value="Black" />
                <Setter Property="FontSize" Value="Medium" />
                <Setter Property="FontAttributes"
                    Value="Bold" />
                <Setter Property="HorizontalTextAlignment"
                    Value="Center" />
                <Setter Property="VerticalTextAlignment"
```

```
                        Value="Center" />
                <Setter Property="VerticalOptions"
                        Value="Center" />
                <Setter Property="HorizontalOptions"
                        Value="End" />
            </Style>
            <Style x:Key="LoginButton" TargetType="Button">
                <Setter Property="BackgroundColor"
                        Value="LightGray" />
                <Setter Property="Margin" Value="0,20,0,0" />
                <Setter Property="TextColor" Value="Black" />
                <Setter Property="WidthRequest" Value="125" />
            </Style>
        </ResourceDictionary>
    </ContentPage.Resources>
```

With the styles in place, we're ready to create the Labels and Entry controls to get a user's name and password:

```
<VerticalStackLayout>
        <Grid
            ColumnDefinitions="*,*,*"
            RowDefinitions="Auto,Auto,Auto,Auto"
            RowSpacing="10">
            <Label
                Grid.Row="0"
                Grid.Column="0"
                Style="{StaticResource Prompt}"
                Text="User name" />
            <Entry
                Grid.Row="0"
                Grid.Column="1"
                Grid.ColumnSpan="2"
                Placeholder="User name"
                Text="{Binding LoginName}"
                WidthRequest="150" />
            <Label
```

```
            Grid.Row="1"
            Grid.Column="0"
            HorizontalOptions="End"
            Style="{StaticResource Prompt}"
            Text="Password" />
        <Entry
            Grid.Row="1"
            Grid.Column="1"
            Grid.ColumnSpan="2"
            IsPassword="True"
            Placeholder="Password"
            Text="{Binding Password}"
            WidthRequest="150" />
        <Button
            Grid.Row="2"
            Grid.Column="0"
            Command="{Binding DoLoginCommand}"
            Style="{StaticResource LoginButton}"
            Text="Submit" />   [2]
```

Once a user has filled in the fields (or is unable to do so because they've forgotten their password), we will offer them the following choices:

```
        <Button
            Grid.Row="2"
            Grid.Column="1"
            Command="{Binding DoCreateAccountCommand}"
            Style="{StaticResource LoginButton}"
            Text="Create Account" /> [3]
        <Button
            Grid.Row="2"
            Grid.Column="2"
            BackgroundColor="LightGray"
            Command="{Binding ForgotPasswordCommand}"
            Style="{StaticResource LoginButton}"
            Text="Forgot Password" /> [4]
    </Grid>
```

```
            <ActivityIndicator    [6]
                x:Name="activityIndicator"
                HeightRequest="50"
                IsRunning="{Binding ShowActivityIndicator}"
                Color="Blue" />

        </VerticalStackLayout>
    </ContentPage>
```

[1] I've expanded the two styles a bit to minimize the styling in the controls.

[2] Click **Submit** to submit the username and password to the API (as we'll see in `ViewModel` a little later).

[3] Click **Create Account** to go to the `CreateAccount` page.

[4] Forgot password is (as they say) left as an exercise for you.

With this new API-oriented **Login** page, we need to update `LoginViewModel`.

The AccountService class

Before updating `LoginViewModel`, we'll need to create the `AccountService` class and its associated interface:

```
using ForgetMeNot.Api.Dto;
using ForgetMeNot.ApiClient;
using System;
using System.Collections.Generic;
using System.Linq;
using System.Text;
using System.Threading.Tasks;


namespace ForgetMeNotDemo.Services
{
  public class AccountService : IAccountService
  {
    readonly Client apiClient;

    public AccountService(Client apiClient)
    {
```

```
        this.apiClient = apiClient;
    }

    public async Task CreateAccount(AccountCreateRequest
      accountCreateRequest)
    {
        await apiClient.CreateAccount(accountCreateRequest);
    }

    public async Task GetNewPassword()
    {
    }

    public async Task Login(LoginRequest request)
    {
        await apiClient.Login(request);
    }

    public bool IsLoggedIn()
    {
        return apiClient.IsAuthenticated;
    }

    }
}
```

This class is used in the creation and authentication of the account. With this in place, we are ready to update LoginViewModel.

Updating LoginViewModel

LoginViewModel must be updated to meet the new requirements of the updated LoginPage class. Once again, delete all that you have and replace it with this:

```
using CommunityToolkit.Mvvm.ComponentModel;
using CommunityToolkit.Mvvm.Input;
using ForgetMeNot.API.Dto;
using ForgetMeNotDemo.Services;
```

```
using ForgetMeNotDemo;

namespace ForgetMeNotDemo.ViewModel
{
  [ObservableObject]
  public partial class LoginViewModel
  {
    private AccountService;                [1]
    [ObservableProperty] private string loginName;
    [ObservableProperty] private string password;
    [ObservableProperty] private bool showActivityIndicator
      = false;
```

The constructor is passed by AccountService by way of the **Inversion of Control (IoC)** container and holds onto that service for its other methods:

```
    public LoginViewModel(AccountService accountService)
      [2]
    {
      this.accountService = accountService;
    }



    [RelayCommand]
    public async Task DoLogin()
    {

      try
      {
        LoginRequest loginRequest = new LoginRequest [3]
        {
          Username = LoginName,
          Password = Password
        };
```

We'll set `ActivityIndicator` to display while we ask the API to log a user in:

```
        ShowActivityIndicator = true;
        await accountService.Login(loginRequest); [4]
        ShowActivityIndicator = false;

        if (accountService.IsLoggedIn()) [5]
        {
          Application.Current.MainPage = new AppShell();
          await Shell.Current.GoToAsync("mainpage");
        }
        else [6]
        {

          await Application.Current.MainPage.DisplayAlert
            ("Login failure",
              "Your username and password do not match our
              records", "Ok");

        }

      }
      catch (Exception exception)
      {
        await Application.Current.MainPage.DisplayAlert
          ("Authorization failure",
            "Your username and password do not match our
            records", "Ok");

        Console.WriteLine(exception);
      }
```

Implementing the logic to manage a forgotten password is left as an exercise for you:

```
    }

    [RelayCommand]
    public async Task ForgotPassword()
```

```
    {
[7]
    }
```

We delegate to the server the responsibility for creating new accounts:

```
    [RelayCommand]
    public async Task DoCreateAccount() [8]
    {
      try
      {
        Application.Current.MainPage = new AppShell();

        await Shell.Current.GoToAsync($"createaccount");

      }
      catch (Exception e)
      {
        Console.WriteLine(e);
      }
    }
}
```

[1] We create the AccountService field, which will mediate between ViewModel and the Client class.

[2] The IoC passes in the AccountService we need, which we will assign to the AccountService member we just created.

[3] We bundle up the username and password into a LoginRequest object. We get this class from ForgetMeNot.API.DTO:

```
public class LoginRequest
{
    public string Username { get; set; }
    public string Password { get; set; }
}
```

[4] We turn `ActivityIndicator` on, pass `LoginRequest` to the API, and then, when we get a response, turn `ActivityIndicator` off. We'll look at what `AccountService` is actually doing in the next step.

[5] We ask `AccountService` whether the login was successful. If it was (the happy path), we reset `MainPage` (away from `LoginPage`) and navigate there.

[6] If login fails (the sad path), we inform the user that we are unable to log them in and give them another chance to do so.

[7] This book will not implement the code to reset a password.

`AccountService` was responsible for the login. Let's look at that next.

Using AccountService to log in

For security purposes, we want a server to be responsible for authenticating a user based on an email address and password:

```
public async Task Login(LoginRequest request)  [1]
{
    await apiClient.Login(request);
}

public bool IsLoggedIn()  [2]
{
    return apiClient.IsAuthenticated;
}
```

Among other methods in `AccountService` (which we will return to shortly) are the following two methods:

[1] Login simply delegates to `apiClient` the responsibility to handle the *login* through the *API*, passing in `LoginRequest`, which contains the username and password.

[2] Similarly, the `IsLoggedIn` Boolean method uses `apiClient` to see whether the current user is *authenticated*.

A second option exists for a user, which is to tap on the **Create Account** button. This brings us to `CreateAccountPage`.

Setting up the Create Account page

The **Create Account** page prompts a user for a username and a password, as well as their email. To keep things simple, in this example, we only ask for the password once, but we do implement validation:

```xml
<?xml version="1.0" encoding="utf-8" ?>
<ContentPage
    x:Class="ForgetMeNotDemo.View.CreateAccountPage"
    xmlns="http://schemas.microsoft.com/dotnet/2021/maui"
    xmlns:x="http://schemas.microsoft.com/winfx/2009/xaml"
    xmlns:behaviors="http://schemas.microsoft.com/dotnet/
      2022/maui/toolkit"
    Title="CreateAccount">
    <VerticalStackLayout>
        <Entry
            HorizontalOptions="FillAndExpand"
            Keyboard="Text"
            Placeholder="Enter Name"
            Text="{Binding Name}">
            <Entry.Behaviors>
                <behaviors:UserStoppedTypingBehavior
                Command="{Binding  ValidateNameCommand}"
                StoppedTypingTimeThreshold="500" />   [1]
            </Entry.Behaviors>
        </Entry>
```

[1] We use the Community Toolkit's `StoppedTypingBehavior` to detect when a user has finished entering a field. We set `StoppedTypingTimeThreshold` to `500` – that is, half a second. This indicates that once the user has not entered anything for half a second, we assume they are done and kick in the validation. Note that the command is set to `ValidateNameCommand`. This is handled in `ViewModel` (as shown later) but returns a Boolean, which indicates whether or not the user has entered a valid name:

```xml
        <Label
            FontSize="13"
            IsVisible="{Binding ShowNameErrorMessage}"
              [1]
            Text="{Binding NameErrorMessage}"
```

```
                    TextColor="Red" />


       <Entry
           HorizontalOptions="FillAndExpand"
           Keyboard="Email"
           Placeholder="Enter Email"
           Text="{Binding Email}">
           <Entry.Behaviors>
               <behaviors:UserStoppedTypingBehavior
                  Command="{Binding ValidateEmailCommand}"
                  StoppedTypingTimeThreshold="500" />
                        [2]
           </Entry.Behaviors>
       </Entry>
```

[1] Only show the label if the name validation fails.

[2] Now, do the same for email as you did for the name, calling ValidateEmailCommand when the user stops typing:

```
       <Label
           FontSize="13"
           IsVisible="{Binding ShowEmailErrorMessage}"
           Text="{Binding EmailErrorMessage}"
           TextColor="Red" />


       <Entry
           HorizontalOptions="FillAndExpand"
           IsPassword="True"    [1]
           Keyboard="Default"
           Placeholder="Enter Password"
           Text="{Binding Password}">
           <Entry.Behaviors>
               <behaviors:UserStoppedTypingBehavior
                  Command="{Binding ValidatePasswordCommand}"
                  StoppedTypingTimeThreshold="500" />
           </Entry.Behaviors>
```

```
        </Entry>
        <Label
            FontSize="13"
            IsVisible="{Binding ShowPasswordErrorMessage}"
            Text="{Binding PasswordErrorMessage}"
            TextColor="Red" />
        <Button
            Margin="0,30,0,0"
            BackgroundColor="LightGray"
            Command="{Binding SignUpCommand}" [2]
            CornerRadius="5"
            HorizontalOptions="Center"
            IsEnabled="{Binding EnableButton}"
            Text="Sign up"
            TextColor="Black"
            TextTransform="None"
            WidthRequest="100" />
    </VerticalStackLayout>
</ContentPage>
```

[1] The IsPassword property of the entry is set to true, and the password will be displayed as a series of asterisks as a user enters a character.

[2] Once the fields are valid, the **Signup** Button will be enabled, and tapping it will invoke the Signup command.

All of the supporting commands and validation are in CreateAccountViewModel.

Setting up CreateAccountViewModel

The first thing we see in this file are all the properties:

```
[ObservableProperty] accountService;
[ObservableProperty] private string name;
[ObservableProperty] private string email;
[ObservableProperty] private string password;
[ObservableProperty] private string nameErrorMessage;
[ObservableProperty] private string emailErrorMessage;
[ObservableProperty] private string passwordErrorMessage;
```

```
[ObservableProperty] private bool showNameErrorMessage;
[ObservableProperty] private bool showEmailErrorMessage;
[ObservableProperty] private bool showPasswordErrorMessage;
[ObservableProperty] private bool enableButton;
[ObservableProperty] private bool isValidName;
[ObservableProperty] private bool isValidEmail;
[ObservableProperty] private bool isValidPassword;
```

Note that there are properties for the error messages along with the prompts. There is also a Boolean property, EnableButton, which defaults to false (if you don't set a Boolean, it defaults to false).

The constructor takes AccountService, passed in by the IoC (this was registered in MauiProgram. cs). Update the Client constructor to take a string serving as baseUrl:

```
var apiClient = new Client("https://forgetmenotapi
    20230113114628.azurewebsites.net/");
builder.Services.AddSingleton(apiClient);


builder.Services.AddTransient<AccountService>();
```

We'll turn to the CreateAccountViewModel class:

```
public CreateAccountViewModel(AccountService
    accountService)
{
    this.accountService = accountService;
}
```

Let's examine a Validation method.

The business requirement is that a valid name has at least two characters. The code to validate is a simple if statement, as follows:

```
[RelayCommand]
public Task ValidateName()
{
    if (!string.IsNullOrEmpty(Name) && Name.Length >= 2)
    {
        IsValidName = true;
        ShowNameErrorMessage = false;
```

```
        EnableButton = IsValidName && IsValidEmail &&
            IsValidPassword; [1]
    }
    else
    {
        NameErrorMessage = "*Please enter a name with at least
            two characters";
        IsValidName = false;
        ShowNameErrorMessage = true;   [2]
        EnableButton = IsValidName && IsValidEmail &&
            IsValidPassword;
    }

    return Task.CompletedTask;
}
```

[1] The `EnableButton` property (which is used to determine whether the **Submit** button is enabled) is only set as `true` when the name, email, and password are all valid.

[2] If the name is not valid, the `ShowNameErrorMessage` property is set to `true`, and the error message is displayed.

In the next chapter, we'll look at the support that .NET MAUI provides for a more elegant validation approach.

The most important command in this file is the one that responds to `SignUpCommand`.

Handling the SignUp command

The `SignUp` method checks to ensure that the fields are valid (by making sure `EnableButton` is true) and then creates an `AccountCreateRequest` object, which is defined in `ForgetMeNot.Api.Dto`:

```
public class AccountCreateRequest
{
    public string FullName { get; set; }
    public string Email { get; set; }
    public string PlainPassword { get; set; }
}
```

It passes that object to the `CreateAccount` method on `accountService`. Let's look at the entire method in `ForgetMeNot.Api.Dto AccountCreateRequest`:

```
[RelayCommand]
async Task SignUp()
{
  if (EnableButton)
  {
    AccountCreateRequest = new() [1]
    {
      Email = this.Email,
      FullName = Name,
      PlainPassword = Password
    };

    try
    {
      await accountService.CreateAccount
        (accountCreateRequest); [2]
      await Application.Current.MainPage.DisplayAlert(
        "Sign up  completed",
          "Your user has been created successfully", "Ok");
            [3]
      await Shell.Current.GoToAsync(".."); [4]
    }
    catch (Exception e)
    {
      await Application.Current.MainPage.DisplayAlert("Sign
        up failed",
          "We were not able to create an account with that
            user name", "Ok");
    }
  }

}
```

[1] Start by creating `AccountCreateRequest` object, as explained earlier.

[2] Call `CreateAccount` on the service. We'll look at that method in just a moment.

[3] If everything works, show a dialog box (or, as we did earlier, a toast).

[4] Once a user account has been created, go back a page to the **Login** page.

All that the `CreateAccount` method in `AccountService` does is pass along the `AccountCreateRequest` object to the `apiClient CreateAccount` method.

The mechanisms described here are correct as far as they go, but they do not include the invitation response that the final app should have (a user invites a buddy who then creates an account).

Let's not forget that we originally created `LoginCS` as a way to mimic the XAML in C#. You'll need to fix up `LoginCS` to match the naming conventions in the XAML file or comment it out altogether, as we are not using it.

It's time to run the program and make sure everything we did works. However, sometimes, you will get unexplained build errors when you make this many changes.

What to do if it won't build

Assuming you've checked all your code, it is correct, and you are getting weird build errors (such as `InitializeComponents not found`), it may be time to clean everything out. To do so, close Visual Studio and navigate to the folder where your files are. Delete the `bin` and `obj` directories within each project, as shown in *Figure 10.1*.

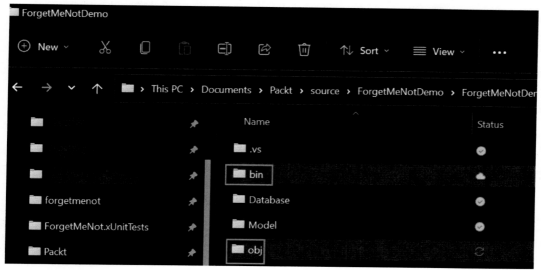

Figure 10.1 – Deleting the bin and obj directories

Follow these steps:

1. Restart Visual Studio and immediately select **Build** | **Clean Solution** from the menu. Finally, select **Build** | **Rebuild Solution**, which forces a complete rebuild rather than an incremental build. Give your project a moment or two to settle down and run it.

   You should be brought directly to the **Login** page, as shown in the following figure:

Figure 10.2 – The Login page

2. Next, click on **Create**, and you'll be brought to the **CreateAccount** page, as shown in *Figure 10.3*. Note that there are no field name prompts on this page; instead, we use the `Placeholder` property of the `Entry` control.

Figure 10.3 – The CreateAccount page

3. Fill in the fields and click **Sign up**. Your account will be created on the server, and a dialog box will appear to let you know it worked, as shown in *Figure 10.4*.

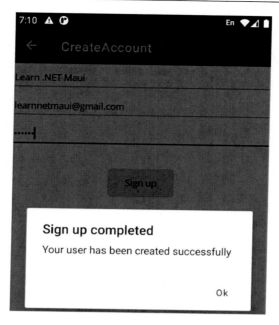

Figure 10.4 – A successful sign-up

If you try to log in, you will get an `unauthorized` message. The problem is that the system does not want the username; it wants the user's email.

> **Unauthorized**
>
> You will, of course, get an unauthorized message with any bad username or invalid password.

Let's fix `LoginPage.xaml` and log in, as shown in *Figure 10.5*.

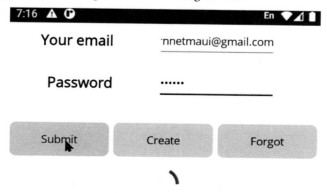

Figure 10.5 – Logging in with our new account

When the login is authenticated, you are taken directly to the home page.

It is important to note and revel in the fact that the account creation and the authentication both take place in the cloud via the API.

Summary

In this chapter, we reviewed how to interact with an API. We gained insight into the internals of that interaction by examining the API domain and DTO projects, and we saw how the `APIClient` class wraps all the API calls to make life easier and more intuitive on the client side.

This is a reasonably advanced topic, and in the next chapter, we will dive into even more advanced topics to move you from being a novice .NET MAUI programmer to an expert.

Quiz

1. What is a DTO?
2. Why don't we need a local SQLite database?
3. What does the API Client class do?
4. Where does account creation occur?
5. Where does authentication occur?

You try it

Implement the *Forgot Password* client-side code.

11
Exploring Advanced Topics

You now have the knowledge and skills of an intermediate .NET MAUI programmer. You've seen how to lay out controls and manage and manipulate those controls. You then learned about the MVVM design pattern. These are the fundamentals.

After that, you advanced to Shell navigation, using SQLite for data persistence and the all-important skill of writing unit tests with mocks.

This final chapter will take you beyond that level into the realm of expert .NET MAUI knowledge. In this chapter, we will cover the following topics:

- Selecting data templates at runtime
- Managing visual state
- Utilizing Community Toolkit behaviors
- Taking action with triggers
- Validating forms

Technical requirements

The source code for this chapter can be found at https://github.com/PacktPublishing/.NET-MAUI-for-C-Sharp-Developers/tree/AdvancedTopics. If you wish to follow along, be sure to use the code from the previous chapter.

Selecting data templates at runtime

You saw data templates in use with collection views in *Chapter 5*. Let's revisit that code and expand upon it to allow us to modify the display of each object at runtime, based on the data in the object itself.

To recap, we started with `PreferenceService`, where we mocked getting a list of `Preference` objects. Now, we can get that from the API, with just a little work. Modify `IPreferenceService` to remove `GetPreferencesMock`.

Next, we need to significantly rework `PreferenceService` to interact with the client. Delete what you have and use the following:

```
using ForgetMeNot.ApiClient;
using ForgetMeNotDemo.Model;

namespace ForgetMeNotDemo.Services;

public class PreferenceService : IPreferenceService
{
  readonly Client apiClient;

  public PreferenceService(Client apiClient)
  {
    this.apiClient = apiClient;
  }
  public async Task<List<Preference>> GetPreferences()
  {
    try
    {
      var response = await apiClient.GetProfile();
      return response?.Preferences.Select(p => new
        Preference
      {
        PreferencePrompt = p.PreferencePrompt,
        PreferenceValue = p.PreferenceValue

      }).ToList();
    }
    catch (Exception e)
    {
      await Application.Current.MainPage.DisplayAlert
        ("Preferences error",
```

```
            "We were unable to get your preferences", "Ok");

        Console.WriteLine(e);
    }


    return null;


    }

}
```

There's nothing new here; it is directly parallel to what we saw in *Chapter 10* when obtaining the *Buddies*. Now that we have a collection of `Preference` objects, we can display them in a `CollectionView`, just as we did in *Chapter 5* (as shown here in `PreferencesPage`, as seen in the previous chapter):

```
<CollectionView
    ItemsSource="{Binding PreferenceList}"
    Margin="20,20,10,10"
    SelectionMode="None">
    <CollectionView.ItemTemplate>
        <DataTemplate>
            <Grid ColumnDefinitions="*,2*">
                <Entry
                    FontSize="10"
                    Grid.Column="0"
                    HorizontalOptions="Start"
                    HorizontalTextAlignment="Start"
                    Text="{Binding PreferencePrompt,
                        Mode=TwoWay}"
                    TextColor="{OnPlatform Black,
                                        iOS=White}" />
                <Entry
                    FontSize="10"
                    Grid.Column="1"
                    HeightRequest="32"
                    HorizontalOptions="Start"
                    HorizontalTextAlignment="Start"
```

```
                        Text="{Binding PreferenceValue,
                            Mode=TwoWay}"
                        TextColor="{OnPlatform Black,
                                            iOS=White}"
                        WidthRequest="350" />
                </Grid>
            </DataTemplate>
        </CollectionView.ItemTemplate>
    </CollectionView>
```

Notice that the CollectionView's `ItemTemplate` is declared *inline*, in the declaration of `CollectionView` itself. That is not the only way to declare an `ItemTemplate`, however. Let's see how to do it another way.

Declaring ItemTemplates as resources

You can take `ItemTemplate` out of the definition of `CollectionView` and move it up into a `ResourceDictionary`:

```
<ContentPage.Resources>   [1]
    <ResourceDictionary>
        <DataTemplate x:Key="PreferenceTemplate"> [2]
            <Grid ColumnDefinitions="*,2*"> [3]
                <Entry
                    FontSize="10"
                    Grid.Column="0"
                    HorizontalOptions="Start"
                    HorizontalTextAlignment="Start"
                    Text="{Binding PreferencePrompt,
                        Mode=TwoWay}"
                    TextColor="{OnPlatform Black,
                            iOS=White}" />
                <Entry
                    FontSize="10"
                    Grid.Column="1"
                    HeightRequest="32"
                    HorizontalOptions="Start"
                    HorizontalTextAlignment="Start"
```

```
                    Text="{Binding PreferenceValue,
                        Mode=TwoWay}"
                    TextColor="{OnPlatform Black,
                                    iOS=White}"
                    WidthRequest="350" />
            </Grid>
        </DataTemplate>
    </ResourceDictionary>
</ContentPage.Resources>
```

Let's look at what we've done here:

- [1]: At the top of the file, we declared a Resources section with a ResourceDictionary
- [2]: We created DataTemplate and gave it a key so that we can refer to it later
- [3]: The rest of DataTemplate is just as it was inside CollectionView

CollectionView is now much simpler – it simply declares its ItemTemplate property to be our created StaticResource:

```
<CollectionView
    ItemsSource="{Binding PreferenceList}"
    ItemTemplate="{StaticResource PreferenceTemplate}"
    Margin="20,20,10,10"
    SelectionMode="None">
</CollectionView>
```

This is valuable but is hardly all that exciting except that it opens up a new possibility.

> **Where to put the DataTemplate**
>
> Here, we show DataTemplate in the resources section, but you can put it in a different file as well.

The DataTemplate selection

You can create two or more additional DataTemplates in the same ResourceDictionary. This allows you to have .NET MAUI examine each *item* as it is about to display it and choose among the available DataTemplates based on a condition.

We know that when we get the preferences, some will have values and some will not. Let's say we want to tell the user to enter a value by turning the prompt red when the value is empty. We can create two DataTemplates:

```xml
<ContentPage.Resources>
    <ResourceDictionary>
        <DataTemplate x:Key="PreferenceTemplate">   [1]
            <Grid ColumnDefinitions="*,2*">
                <Entry
                    FontSize="10"
                    Grid.Column="0"
                    HorizontalOptions="Start"
                    HorizontalTextAlignment="Start"
                    Text="{Binding PreferencePrompt,
                        Mode=TwoWay}"
                    TextColor="{OnPlatform Black,    [2]
                                    iOS=White}" />
                <Entry
                    FontSize="10"
                    Grid.Column="1"
                    HeightRequest="32"
                    HorizontalOptions="Start"
                    HorizontalTextAlignment="Start"
                    Text="{Binding PreferenceValue,
                        Mode=TwoWay}"
                    TextColor="{OnPlatform Black,
                                        iOS=White}"
                    WidthRequest="350" />
            </Grid>
        </DataTemplate>
        <DataTemplate x:Key=
            "PreferenceTemplateEmpty">
            [3]
            <Grid ColumnDefinitions="*,2*">
                <Entry
                    FontSize="10"
                    Grid.Column="0"
                    HorizontalOptions="Start"
                    HorizontalTextAlignment="Start"
                    Text="{Binding PreferencePrompt,
```

```
                          Mode=TwoWay}"
                   TextColor="{OnPlatform Red,
                              iOS=Yellow}" />        [4]
               <Entry
                   FontSize="10"
                   Grid.Column="1"
                   HeightRequest="32"
                   HorizontalOptions="Start"
                   HorizontalTextAlignment="Start"
                   Text="{Binding PreferenceValue,
                       Mode=TwoWay}"
                   TextColor="{OnPlatform Black,
                                      iOS=White}"
                   WidthRequest="350" />
           </Grid>
        </DataTemplate>
       </ResourceDictionary>
     </ContentPage.Resources>
```

Let's take a look at this:

- [1]: The first data template
- [2]: The normal text colors
- [3]: The second data template (with its own key)
- [4]: The *empty* text colors

Now, the obvious question is, how does .NET MAUI know which to display? For that, we need a DataTemplateSelector.

The DataTemplateSelector class

The first thing you must do is create a class that will contain the logic as to which template to display. I've named that class PreferenceDataTemplateSelector. Since I only intend to have one, I put it in the Services folder:

```
using ForgetMeNotDemo.Model;

namespace ForgetMeNotDemo.Services;

public class PreferenceDataTemplateSelector :
```

```
  DataTemplateSelector   [1]
{

  public DataTemplate PreferenceTemplate { get; set; }
    [2]
  public DataTemplate PreferenceTemplateEmpty { get; set; }

  protected override DataTemplate OnSelectTemplate(object
    item,   [3] BindableObject container)
  {
    if (((Preference)item)?.PreferenceValue == null)
      return PreferenceTemplateEmpty;
    return ((Preference) item).PreferenceValue.Length > 0 ?
      PreferenceTemplate : PreferenceTemplateEmpty;   [4]
  }
}
```

You must do the following:

[1]: Your class must derive from `DataTemplateSelector`.

[2]: You need a public property for each of your DataTemplates.

[3]: Override the `OnSelectTemplate` virtual method.

[4]: Add the logic as to which template to display.

With the class in place, we need to have a corresponding resource.

Adding the template selector to the page's resources

Return to `PreferencesPage.xaml`. In the page declaration, add `Xmlns:services="clr-namespace:ForgetMeNotDemo.Services"`. Then, in `ResourceDictionary`, add the following:

```
<services:PreferenceDataTemplateSelector
            PreferenceTemplate="{StaticResource
                PreferenceTemplate}"
            PreferenceTemplateEmpty="{StaticResource
                PreferenceTemplateEmpty}"
            x:Key="PreferenceDataTemplateSelector" />
```

This provides the link to the names in the class we just created. We now have the logic, but how do we hook it up to `CollectionView`?

Adding DataTemplateSelector to CollectionView

Hooking all this into `CollectionView` is as simple as setting an `ItemTemplate`:

```
<CollectionView
    ItemTemplate="{StaticResource PreferenceDataTemplate
        Selector}"
    ItemsSource="{Binding PreferenceList}"
    Margin="20,20,10,10"
    SelectionMode="None" />
```

And it all comes together. `CollectionView` looks to `PreferenceDataTemplateSelector` in the resources, which is tied to the class we created that holds the logic as to which `DataTemplate` to show. The result is shown in *Figure 11.1*:

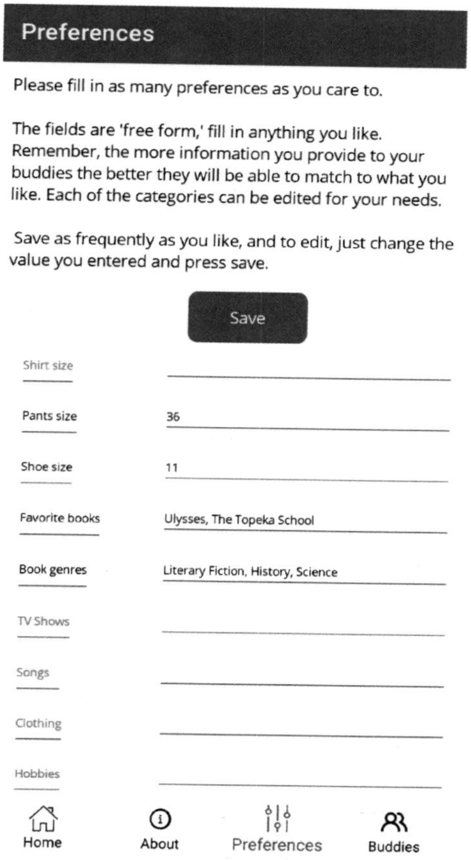

Figure 11.1 – DataTemplate selection

`DataTemplateSelector` is a very powerful way to control what is displayed at runtime. A similar mechanism is encapsulated in the concept of Visual State.

Managing Visual State

Every `VisualElement` has a *Visual State* at any given moment (for example, does `VisualElement` have *focus*? Is it *selected*?). You can imagine responding to that state programmatically in C#, but there are advantages to responding to changes in visual state declaratively, in the XAML. Doing so puts more of the UI management in one place – your view (for example, `MainPage.xaml`).

> **VisualElement**
> `VisualElement` is the base class of all controls (and pages).

The object that sets visual properties on `VisualElement` based on its state is the **Visual State Manager**. The Visual State Manager selects from among a set of `VisualStates` and displays a `VisualElement` according to the properties set in the XAML.

This forces the question: what are visual states?

Defining the common visual states

.NET MAUI defines a set of common visual states:

- `Normal`
- `Disabled`
- `Has focus`
- `Is selected`
- `Mouse over` (for Windows and macOS)

.NET MAUI also allows you to define your own visual states, though that is less common.

You use these visual states to set properties on `VisualElement`. For example, you might change the appearance of a button based on its `VisualState`. An example will make this much clearer.

A button VisualState example

When you first go to the **Login** page, you will see that the **Submit** button is disabled. We'd like it to be gray. Once you fill in the **Your Email** and **Password** fields, the button should turn light green. If you tab to the button, it should signify that it has the focus by turning fully green. You can do all this declaratively by creating visual states, as shown in *Figure 11.2*:

Figure 11.2 – Visual states of buttons

You can set the visual state on an individual button, or, as we will do here, you can put the visual state's XAML into a style and apply it to all the buttons. Here is the complete Style for buttons:

```
<Style x:Key="LoginButton" TargetType="Button"> [1]
    <Setter Property="Margin" Value="0,20,0,0" />
    <Setter Property="TextColor" Value="Black" />
    <Setter Property="WidthRequest" Value="125" />
    <Setter Property="VisualStateManager
      .VisualStateGroups"> [2]
        <VisualStateGroupList>
            <VisualStateGroup x:Name="CommonStates"> [3]
                <VisualState x:Name="Normal"> [4]
                    <VisualState.Setters> [5]
                        <Setter Property="BackgroundColor"
                            Value="LightGreen" /> [6]
                    </VisualState.Setters>
                </VisualState>
                <VisualState x:Name="Focused">
                    <VisualState.Setters>
                        <Setter Property="BackgroundColor"
                            Value="Green" />
                    </VisualState.Setters>
                </VisualState>
                <VisualState x:Name="Disabled">
                    <VisualState.Setters>
                        <Setter Property="BackgroundColor"
                            Value="Gray" />
```

```
                    </VisualState.Setters>
                </VisualState>
            </VisualStateGroup>
        </VisualStateGroupList>
    </Setter>
</Style>
```

Here, we have the following:

- [1]: We start by declaring a normal Style – in this case, it's implicit for every button
- [2]: You may have one or more groups of visual states (we have one)
- [3]: The first group (and in this case, the only one) is CommonStates
- [4]: We declare each VisualState in turn (here, we're starting with Normal)
- [5]: For each state, we can declare a set of Setters
- [6]: Our first (and in this case, only) Setter sets the BackgroundColor property

We then go on to set the Setters for all the other states. Notice that we did not set a Setter for PointerOver, which means that, on Windows and macOS, if you hover the mouse over the button, there will be no change.

.NET MAUI defines specialized visual states for controls. For example, Button adds the *Pressed* state, while CheckBox adds the *IsChecked* state and CollectionViews adds *Selected*.

The .NET MAUI Community Toolkit provides further help for managing the appearance and behavior of your app with a large collection of behaviors.

Utilizing Community Toolkit behaviors

We've already seen one *behavior* from the *Community Toolkit* that turns an event into a command (EventToCommandBehavior), allowing us to respond to these events in our ViewModel.

> **The Community Toolkit is open source**
> The Community Toolkit is not officially part of .NET MAUI and consists of code supplied by (surprise!) the community – that is, developers independent of Microsoft. That said, the Microsoft documentation includes and increasingly integrates the Community Toolkit.

CommunityToolkit provides a suite of behaviors to handle many other common programming needs. Many of these behaviors assist with validating input. For example, the CommunityToolkit includes the following:

- Character validation
- Numeric validation
- Required string validation
- Text validation
- URI validation

You attach behaviors to controls. For example, let's add a rule to the **Login** page stating that the username must be a valid email address. First, in the header, add the needed namespace:

```
Xmlns:behaviors=
http://schemas.microsoft.com/dotnet/2022/maui/toolkit
```

You are then ready to test for a valid email using the Community Toolkit behavior:

```
<Entry
    Grid.Column="1"
    Grid.ColumnSpan="2"
    Grid.Row="0"
    Placeholder="Please enter your email address"
    Text="{Binding LoginName}"
    WidthRequest="150">
    <Entry.Behaviors>    [1]
        <behaviors:EmailValidationBehavior    [2]
            InvalidStyle="{StaticResource InvalidUserName}"
            [3]
            ValidStyle="{StaticResource ValidUserName}" [4]
            Flags="ValidateOnValueChanged" /> [5]
    </Entry.Behaviors>
</Entry>
```

Do the following:

[1]: Begin the Behaviors section of the Entry tag.

[2]: Choose which behavior you want (in this case, email validation).

[3]: Identify the style for an invalid email address.

[4]: Identify the style for a valid email address.

[5]: Add validation behaviors. They have flags to indicate when to do the validation (in this case, when the value changes), as shown in the following figure:

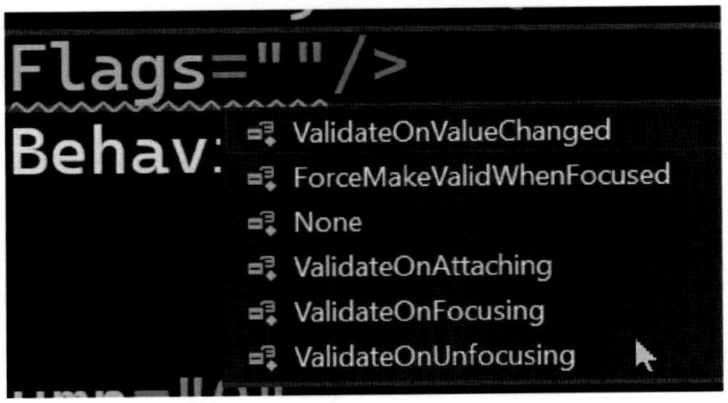

Figure 11.3 – Validation flags

There are several other non-validating behaviors as well. These include behaviors to assist with animating views, progress bar animation, a behavior to assist with customizing the color and style of your device's status bar, and a behavior to trigger an action when the user stops typing.

The last of these can be very helpful when allowing the user to search a large set of data. Rather than having the search be incremental as the user types, or forcing the user to tap a **Search** button, you can have the search begin when the user stops typing for a specified period:

```
Place the following code at the top of PreferencesPage.xaml

<Entry Placeholder="Search" x:Name="SearchEntry">
    <Entry.Behaviors>
        <behaviors:UserStoppedTypingBehavior
            Command="{Binding PreferencesSearchCommand}"
            [1]
            CommandParameter="{Binding Source={x:Reference
                SearchEntry}, Path=Text}"    [2]
            MinimumLengthThreshold="4"   [3]
            ShouldDismissKeyboardAutomatically="True" [4]
            StoppedTypingTimeThreshold="500" /> [5]
    </Entry.Behaviors>
</Entry>
```

Let's look at what this code does:

- [1]: When the user stops typing, call this command in your `ViewModel`
- [2]: Pass this parameter (the text of `Entry`) to the command
- [3]: Don't execute the command unless at least this many characters have been entered
- [4]: When you execute the command, put away the keyboard
- [5]: Wait this long (half a second) to indicate the user has stopped typing

When you add this to your XAML, and the user enters `Shoe` in the entry, the command is fired and the parameter is sent. *Figure 11.4* shows the parameter being passed into the command handler in `PreferencesPageViewModel`:

```
[RelayCommand]
2 references | 0 changes | 0 authors, 0 changes
private async Task PreferencesSearch(object param)
{
    // Search for requested string
    var search:string? = param.ToString();    param = "shoe"

}
```

Figure 11.4 – Passing in the search string

Behaviors are a way to declare how the system should perform in XAML. Another powerful mechanism for moving responsive actions into the XAML triggers.

Taking action with triggers

Triggers allow you to declare how a control should appear in your XAML based on data changes. You can also use *state triggers* to change a control's *Visual State*, as shown earlier.

For example, we may want to enforce that the **Create Account** button should be disabled if the user has left the **Password** field blank. You can do this in code, but you can also do it declaratively in XAML using a `DataTrigger`:

```
<Button
    Command="{Binding DoCreateAccountCommand}"
    Grid.Column="1"
    Grid.Row="2"
```

```
    Style="{StaticResource LoginButton}"
    Text="Create Account">
    <Button.Triggers>   [1]
        <DataTrigger
            Binding="{Binding Source={x:Reference
                passwordEntry}, Path=Text.Length}"
            TargetType="Button"
            Value="0">  [2]
            <Setter Property="IsEnabled" Value="False" />
            [3]
        </DataTrigger>
    </Button.Triggers>
</Button>
```

Let's look at what this code does:

- [1]: This starts the Triggers collection of Button.
- [2]: This creates a DataTrigger and sets it to bind to the length of the text in the entry control whose name is passwordEntry. Set TargetType to Button (required) and the value for it to trigger on (that is, if the length of the password entry text is 0, then fire the trigger).
- [3]: This code uses a setter to declare what happens when the trigger fires.

In short, when the **Password** field is empty, the **Create** button should be disabled and as soon as it is not empty, the button should be enabled.

Unexpected behavior

The field you are checking (Password) must have its text initialized to " " for this to work. Otherwise, it will be null and the trigger may not act as expected. To solve this, initialize the property in ViewModel:

```
[observableproperty]
public string password = string.Empty;
```

The result of this trigger is shown in *Figure 11.5* and *Figure 11.6*.

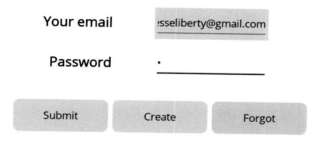

Figure 11.5 – Trigger when the Password field is empty

In *Figure 11.5*, the **Password** field is empty, while in *Figure 11.6*, a character has been typed into the **Password** field:

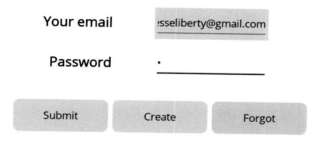

Figure 11.6 – Trigger when the Password field is not empty

For fun, change `Property` from `IsEnabled` to `IsVisible`. Now, the button is not there when you enter the page, but will appear when you put a character into the **Password** field.

Summary

In this chapter, we reviewed four key advanced topics that allow you to manage the behavior of your app declaratively:

- Selecting data templates allows you to change the display of your data based on the specific content of each element in a collection
- Managing the view state allows you to modify the appearance of a control based on the *state* of that control (for example, does it have focus?)
- Behaviors allow, among other things, data validation and otherwise assist in providing actions that you declare

- Triggers change the appearance of controls based on data values in other controls or based on the state of other controls

This brings us to the end of `.Net MAUI for C# Developers`. You are now fully equipped to create real-world professional .NET MAUI applications.

The key to success with .NET MAUI, as with so many programming skills, is hands-on experience. If you are not currently working on a .NET MAUI project, you will want to assign one to yourself while this information is front and center in your mind.

Here's an application idea I've had for years, which you are free to write (and sell if you want). I'll give it to you without restriction:

Create a nice-looking application that gathers all the books on an online bookstore (using their public API) that you rated with five stars. Next, gather all the people who have also rated a large percentage of those books five stars. Exclude anyone who gave any of those books less than five stars. Now, take those people who seem to agree with you, and find any books they rated as five stars that you've not read yet. Those are books you'll want to read.

Enjoy the project! I hope you have enjoyed this book.

Quiz

Answer the following questions to test your knowledge of this chapter:

1. Why would you use the Visual State Manager?
2. How does .NET MAUI decide which data template to use?
3. Name a behavior that is not used for validation.
4. When a trigger fires, how does it know what to do?

You try it

Modify the **Login** page so that it does the following:

- Disables the **Login** button unless the username is a valid email address and the password has at least one character.
- Modifies the **Forgot Password** button to double in size and turn pink when you tab onto it (giving it the focus), and returns to its normal size and color when it loses focus

Assessments

This section contains answers to questions from all chapters.

Chapter 1, Assembling Your Tools and Creating Your First App

1. You can create a new project from the launch dialog by choosing **Create a new project**. If you've been brought directly into Visual Studio, by clicking on **File | New Project**.
2. Use **View | Solution Explorer**.
3. The `.xaml` extension indicates that the file contains XAML markup.
4. The code-behind file.
5. `MauiProgram.cs`.

Chapter 3, XAML and Fluent C#

1. XAML is a markup language based on XML.
2. XAML is used in .NET MAUI for declaring layouts and controls.
3. Rather than writing in XAML, you can create your layouts and controls in C#.
4. We nest a layout or a control inside a layout by using the `Children` property.
5. An event handler is a method that is registered to an event in the UI.
6. The event handler is in the code-behind.

Chapter 4, MVVM and Controls

1. MVVM has two main advantages. First, it is nearly impossible to unit test a .NET MAUI application if your logic is in the code-behind file – putting the logic in `ViewModel` is essential, as we'll see in the upcoming chapter on unit testing. Second, MVVM nicely decouples the UI from your logic, allowing you to change one without breaking the other.
2. The all-important `BindingContext`. You typically assign `ViewModel` as the binding context for `View`.
3. The `Entry` control and the `Editor` control.

4. The `Label` control.

5. `SnackBar` is a highly configurable `Toast` – a popup that comes up from the bottom of the page and then can disappear either by its timer running out or by a user clicking on it.

Chapter 5, Advanced Controls

1. `ActivityIndicator` shows that *something* is happening, while `ProgressBar` tells the user what fraction of the task is complete.

2. The essential difference as far as we are concerned is that events are typically handled in the code-behind, while commands are handled in `ViewModel`. Handling commands in `ViewModel` is preferable because it makes creating unit tests easier or possible.

3. `WeakReferenceManager` is the primary object used in messaging, allowing `ViewModel` to send notifications to `View` or another `ViewModel` without a reference to that object, thus supporting loose coupling.

4. Styles allow you to create a uniform appearance across instances of controls, centralizing the properties and providing all the advantages of well-factored code.

5. One way to refactor styles is to create a base style and then use `BasedOn` to create derived types, adding or overriding properties as needed.

Chapter 6, Layout

1. Stars, `auto`, and the value in dpi

2. Allocate 100 dpi to the last column, the needed size for the second column, and then divide the first and third columns proportionally as 2:1

3. The row and column offsets are defined by enumerated constants

4. `Grid` allows for more precise alignment and placement of controls

5. `BindableLayout` does not allow you to make selections

Chapter 7, Understanding Navigation

1. `AppShell.xaml`

2. `Title`, `ContentTemplate`, and `Icon`

3. `AppShell.xaml.cs`

4. `Shell.Current.GoToAsync`

5. URL syntax or using a dictionary

Chapter 8, Storing and Retrieving Data

1. `Preferences` (not to be confused with `UserPreferences`).
2. The key and a default value.
3. **SQLite-net-pcl** and possibly **SQLitePCLRaw.bundle_green**, if not included with **SQLite-net-pcl**.
4. `SQLiteAsyncConnection`

Chapter 9, Unit Testing

1. Unit tests are critical for ensuring the quality of your code and allow you to add to and change your code with the confidence of knowing that if you break something, you'll find out about it right away.
2. Most of the testable code in a .NET MAUI application will be in the ViewModel or, possibly, the services.
3. When you need a slower service to test a method in your code, a mock can stand in for that service and give you immediate responses.
4. In order to provide a mock to your test, you must be able to inject it into the code in lieu of the runtime object.

Chapter 10, Consuming REST Services

1. A DTO is responsible for holding data that will be sent to and/or from the API.
2. The database is now in the cloud and managed through the API. As the client, we don't know, nor need to know, what kind of database is in use.
3. It wraps all the API calls so that a client can interact with the API as if it were a **Plain Old CLR Object (POCO)**.
4. Account creation is accomplished in the cloud via the API.
5. Authentication is accomplished in the cloud via the API.

Chapter 11, Exploring Advanced Topics

1. To modify the appearance of a control based on its *state*, such as whether or not it has the focus.
2. In the XAML, add a `DataTemplateSelector` to indicate the potential templates and then add a class that derives from `DataTemplateSelector` that overrides `OnSelectTemplate` and returns `DataTemplate` to be displayed.
3. We have seen the `EventToCommand` behavior, which allows you to add commands to controls that only have events, allowing you to handle the event/command in `ViewModel`.
4. You add setters with the property to change and the value to set it to.

Index

Packtpub.com

Subscribe to our online digital library for full access to over 7,000 books and videos, as well as industry leading tools to help you plan your personal development and advance your career. For more information, please visit our website.

Why subscribe?

- Spend less time learning and more time coding with practical eBooks and Videos from over 4,000 industry professionals

- Improve your learning with Skill Plans built especially for you

- Get a free eBook or video every month

- Fully searchable for easy access to vital information

- Copy and paste, print, and bookmark content

Did you know that Packt offers eBook versions of every book published, with PDF and ePub files available? You can upgrade to the eBook version at packtpub.com and as a print book customer, you are entitled to a discount on the eBook copy. Get in touch with us at customercare@packtpub.com for more details.

At www.packtpub.com, you can also read a collection of free technical articles, sign up for a range of free newsletters, and receive exclusive discounts and offers on Packt books and eBooks.

Other Books You May Enjoy

If you enjoyed this book, you may be interested in these other books by Packt:

High-Performance Programming in C# and .NET

Jason Alls

ISBN: 9781800564718

- Use correct types and collections to enhance application performance
- Profile, benchmark, and identify performance issues with the codebase
- Explore how to best perform queries on LINQ to improve an application's performance
- Effectively utilize a number of CPUs and cores through asynchronous programming
- Build responsive user interfaces with WinForms, WPF, MAUI, and WinUI
- Benchmark ADO.NET, Entity Framework Core, and Dapper for data access
- Implement CQRS and event sourcing and build and deploy microservices

Parallel Programming and Concurrency with C# 10 and .NET 6

Alvin Ashcraft

ISBN: 9781803243672

- Prevent deadlocks and race conditions with managed threading
- Update Windows app UIs without causing exceptions
- Explore best practices for introducing asynchronous constructs to existing code
- Avoid pitfalls when introducing parallelism to your code
- Implement the producer-consumer pattern with Dataflow blocks
- Enforce data sorting when processing data in parallel and safely merge data from multiple sources
- Use concurrent collections that help synchronize data across threads
- Debug an everyday parallel app with the Parallel Stacks and Parallel Tasks windows

Packt is searching for authors like you

If you're interested in becoming an author for Packt, please visit `authors.packtpub.com` and apply today. We have worked with thousands of developers and tech professionals, just like you, to help them share their insight with the global tech community. You can make a general application, apply for a specific hot topic that we are recruiting an author for, or submit your own idea.

Share Your Thoughts

Now you've finished *.Net MAUI for C# Developers*, we'd love to hear your thoughts! Scan the QR code below to go straight to the Amazon review page for this book and share your feedback or leave a review on the site that you purchased it from.

`https://packt.link/r/1837631697`

Your review is important to us and the tech community and will help us make sure we're delivering excellent quality content.

Download a free PDF copy of this book

Thanks for purchasing this book!

Do you like to read on the go but are unable to carry your print books everywhere?

Is your eBook purchase not compatible with the device of your choice?

Don't worry, now with every Packt book you get a DRM-free PDF version of that book at no cost.

Read anywhere, any place, on any device. Search, copy, and paste code from your favorite technical books directly into your application.

The perks don't stop there, you can get exclusive access to discounts, newsletters, and great free content in your inbox daily

Follow these simple steps to get the benefits:

1. Scan the QR code or visit the link below

https://packt.link/free-ebook/9781837631698

2. Submit your proof of purchase
3. That's it! We'll send your free PDF and other benefits to your email directly

Made in the USA
Middletown, DE
12 July 2023

34987047R00166